SIGNIFICANCE: the struggle we share

SIGNIFICANCE:

the struggle we share

John H. Brennecke

Robert G. Amick

Mt. San Antonio College

GLENCOE PRESS
A Division of The Macmillan Company
Beverly Hills, California

**For Tori Amick, Jeff and Jim Brennecke—
may they know their personal significance better
because of these efforts.**

Contents

Introduction

Some would call this the age of anxiety; others, the atomic age, the age of aquarius, the technological age. All of these are adequate labels. Each of us might supply his own in addition to these.

Among the most crucial crises confronting human beings in these troubled times is what Rollo May calls the crisis of significance.[1] In another work, *The Struggle for Significance,* we have chronicled the conflict of modern man as he gropes his way out of the welter of confusions and conflicts into the light of self-actualizing fulfillment.

More than feeling lost, alienated, alone, many of us have experienced the desperate feeling of doubt as to our own significance. We may amass money, invent gadgets, accumulate material goods, gain prestige and reputation, seek and find love, and all of these can be good in and of themselves. But many people continue to feel that their own selfhood is unimportant. They find themselves in a battle to declare who they are, hoping for that declaration to make a difference.

To feel significant is not necessarily to become important or famous. Far from it. Most of the people to whom this book is addressed will never become famous or wealthy or powerful. But they can attain a feeling of significant selfhood. They can live their lives in such a full and rewarding way that they will come to know that their being here has mattered, that they have made a ripple on the pond.

---

1. Rollo May, *Psychology and the Human Dilemma* (Princeton: Van Nostrand Co., Inc., 1967).

Too many people, in a million different situations, slough through life, experiencing small satisfactions, gaining slight rewards, knowing some pleasure, but living very dreary lives. We find such people in our classrooms, therapeutic practice, friendships, and acquaintances. They are the stimulation for our work.

In this book, we have tried to gather together the writings of significant writers to illustrate and complement our own views. Not all of these authors are psychologists, nor even connected with the field of mental health. Yet, what they have to say is extremely important and can aid the reader in coming to some understanding of the vastness of the problem. Further, since these articles represent the findings and opinions of people in many different situations and cultures, the reader can gain some comfort and a greater sense of his kinship with other human beings in reading of man's common search.

Some of the readings are fiction. In the selections made from novels or stories, we have found meaningful and vital descriptions of people in their search for significant selfhood. You may not be amused or entertained by all of them, but we feel you'll be enlightened.

How do we express our gratitude to the countless people who have been a part of this? Award winners have almost ruined the art of acknowledgment with silly and superficial speeches. So, to our colleagues, students, clients, friends and families, for all their suggestions, opinions, editorializing, and patience, we simply but sincerely say "Thank you." To the authors whose work we are using, to their publishers, and to our own, we add another very sincere note of appreciation. We hope these authors will feel that we are all joining in a common search. Finally, we wish to acknowledge the great help of Mrs. Velda Galloway of the Mt. San Antonio College Library for her patient work. Our typist, Mrs. Naomi Brooker, has got to be one of the world's finest workers, as well as one of the nicest people. To Bernadette Brennecke and Taffy Amick, our wives, apologies for months of neglect and grateful kisses for patience and love.

John H. Brennecke
Robert G. Amick

SIGNIFICANCE: the struggle we share

The Crisis of Insignificance

Man is born. Man dies. In between, what? Is there a meaning to this round-robin experience called life? The existentialists have made it their entire theme. Beginning with the realization of the fact of death, we are told that we must so shape our lives that we live them—not simply let them be lived. Decision, commitment, and responsibility are the major requirements of meaningful living.

Without doing business with the fact of death, man lives in a fantasy world. We don't expect that a significant human being will spend every waking moment dwelling on his own mortality, but the fully-living person lives with the fact of the shortness of life and lets that reality so pervade his being that he lives his life more fully, more meaningfully, more richly, and certainly more realistically.

Doesn't this lead to gloomy despair? For some, yes. But for the person who knows that death is part of the facts of life, it should be something that takes its place alongside the other facts. Having made realistic room for this reality, he can then take on the other less morbid and less frightening aspects of human existence. Human life can be lived joyfully. If life were *only* a burden, *only* a struggle, *only* an assortment of pains, we'd say, "Hang it up" too! But life can be joyful; human beings can know happiness and a feeling of worth.

We begin with a reference to a very happy man, Alexis Zorba. Nikos Kazantzakis has given the world a story of a full and rich man in *Zorba the Greek*. Zorba, for all his peculiarities and peccadilloes, is a fully human and large-living man, who is flesh-and-blood to millions of people, including us.

The second reading is another fiction piece. Albert Camus, in *The Stranger*, introduces us to the existential posture in literature, inviting each reader to find his own kinship with the hero, Meursault.

from *Zorba the Greek*

Nikos Kazantzakis

A young man, half Greek and half English, returns to take possession of his inheritance: a lignite mine on the Greek isle of Crete. He meets a rascally jack-of-all-trades, Alexis Zorba, who promises not only to show him how to re-open the mine and make his fortune, but also how to get a bit more out of life. The scholarly, shy little fellow falls into many philosophical discussions with the rough but deep-feeling old worker. In the following excerpts, Zorba and his "boss" are discussing the matter of man's existence on earth.

"You don't believe in man, do you?" I retorted.

"Now, don't get angry, boss. No, I don't believe in anything. If I believed in man, I'd believe in God, and I'd believe in the devil, too. And that's a whole business. Things get all muddled then, boss, and cause me a lot of complications."

He became silent, took off his beret, scratched his head frantically and tugged again at his moustache, as if he meant to tear it off. He wanted to say something, but he restrained himself. He looked at me out of the corner of his eye; looked at me again and decided to speak.

"Man is a brute," he said, striking the pebbles with his stick. "A great brute. Your lordship doesn't realize this. It seems everything's been too easy for you, but you ask me! A brute, I tell you! If you're cruel to him, he respects and fears you. If you're kind to him, he plucks your eyes out.

"Keep your distance, boss! Don't make men too bold, don't go telling them we're all equal, we've got the same rights, or they'll go straight and trample on *your* rights; they'll steal your bread and leave you to die of hunger. Keep your distance, boss, by all the good things I wish you!"

"But don't you believe in anything?" I exclaimed in exasperation.

"No, I don't believe in anything. How many times must I tell you that? I don't believe in anything or anyone; only in Zorba. Not because Zorba is better than the others; not at all, not a little bit! He's a brute like the rest! But I believe in Zorba because he's the only being I have in my power, the only one I know. All the rest are ghosts. I see with these eyes, I hear with these ears, I digest with these guts. All the rest are ghosts, I tell you. When I die, everything'll die. The whole Zorbatic world will go to the bottom!"

"What egoism!" I said sarcastically.

"I can't help it, boss! That's how it is. I eat beans, I talk beans; I am Zorba, I talk like Zorba."

I said nothing. Zorba's words stung me like whiplashes. I admired him for being so strong, for despising men to that extent, and at the same time wanting to live and work with them. I should either have become an ascetic or else have adorned men with false feathers so that I could put up with them.

Zorba looked round at me. By the light of the stars I could see he was grinning from ear to ear.

"Have I offended you, boss?" he said, stopping abruptly. We had arrived at the hut. Zorba looked at me tenderly and uneasily.

I did not reply. I felt my mind was in agreement with Zorba, but my heart resisted, wanted to leap out and escape from the brute, to go its own road.

· · · · · · · · · · · · · · · · ·

When he returned one evening, he asked me anxiously: "Is there a God—yes or no? What d'you think, boss? And if there is one—anything's possible—what d'you think he looks like?"

I shrugged my shoulders.

"I'm not joking, boss. I think of God as being exactly like me. Only bigger, stronger, crazier. And immortal, into the bargain. He's sitting on a pile of soft sheepskins and his hut's the sky. It isn't made out of old petrol-cans, like ours is, but clouds. In his right hand he's holding not a knife or a pair of scales—those damned instruments are meant for butchers and grocers—no, he's holding a large sponge full of water, like a rain-cloud. On his right is Paradise, on his left Hell. Here comes a soul; the poor little thing's quite naked, because it's lost its cloak—its body, I mean—and it's shivering. God looks at it, laughing up his sleeve, but he plays the bogy man: 'Come here,' he roars, 'come here, you miserable wretch!'

"And he begins his questioning. The naked soul throws itself at God's feet. 'Mercy!' it cries. 'I have sinned.' And away it goes reciting its sins. It recites a whole rigmarole and there's no end to it. God thinks this is too much of a good thing. He yawns. 'For heaven's sake stop!' he shouts. 'I've heard enough of all that!' Flap! Slap! a wipe of the sponge, and he washes out all the sins. 'Away with you, clear out, run off to Paradise!' he says to the soul. 'Peterkin, let this poor little creature in, too!'

"Because God, you know, is a great lord, and that's what being a lord means: to forgive!"

I remember I had to laugh that evening, while Zorba was pouring out his profound balderdash. But this "lordliness" of God was taking shape and maturing within me, compassionate, generous and all-powerful.

.   .   .   .

A moment later he decided to speak.

"Can you tell me, boss," he said, and his voice sounded deep and earnest in the warm night, "what all these things mean? Who made them all? And why? And, above all"—here Zorba's voice trembled with anger and fear—"why do people die?"

"I don't know, Zorba," I replied, ashamed, as if I had been asked the simplest thing, the most essential thing, and was unable to explain it.

"You don't know!" said Zorba in round-eyed astonishment, just like his expression the night I had confessed I could not dance.

He was silent a moment and then suddenly broke out.

"Well, all those damned books you read—what good are they? Why do you read them? If they don't tell you that, what *do* they tell you?"

"They tell me about the perplexity of mankind, who can give no answer to the question you've just put me, Zorba."

"Oh, damn their perplexity!" he cried, tapping his foot on the ground in exasperation.

The parrot started up at these noises.

"Canavaro! Canavaro!" he called, as if for help.

"Shut up! You, too!" shouted Zorba, banging on the cage with his fist.

He turned back to me.

"I want you to tell me where we come from and where we are going to. During all those years you've been burning yourself up consuming their black books of magic, you must have chewed over about fifty tons of paper! What did you get out of them?"

There was so much anguish in his voice that my heart was wrung with distress. Ah! how I would have liked to be able to answer him!

I felt deep within me that the highest point a man can attain is not Knowledge, or Virtue, or Goodness, or Victory, but something even greater, more heroic and more despairing: Sacred Awe!

"Can't you answer?" asked Zorba anxiously.

I tried to make my companion understand what I meant by Sacred Awe.

"We are little grubs, Zorba, minute grubs on the small leaf of a tremendous tree. This small leaf is the earth. The other leaves are the stars that you see moving at night. We make our way on this little leaf examining it anxiously and carefully. We smell it; it smells good or bad to us. We taste it and find it eatable. We beat on it and it cries out like a living thing.

"Some men—the more intrepid ones—reach the edge of the leaf. From there we stretch out, gazing into chaos. We tremble. We guess what a frightening abyss lies beneath us. In the distance we can hear the noise of the other leaves of the tremendous tree, we feel the sap rising from the roots to our leaf and our hearts swell. Bent thus over the awe-inspiring abyss, with all our bodies and all our souls, we tremble with terror. From that moment begins . . ."

I stopped. I wanted to say "from that moment begins poetry," but Zorba would not have understood. I stopped.

"What begins?" asked Zorba's anxious voice. "Why did you stop?"

". . . begins the great danger, Zorba. Some grow dizzy and delirious, others are afraid; they try to find an answer to strengthen their hearts, and they say: 'God!' Others again, from the edge of the leaf, look over the precipice calmly and bravely and say: 'I like it.' "

Zorba reflected for a long time. He was straining to understand.

"You know," he said at last, "I think of death every second. I look at it and I'm not frightened. But never, never, do I say I like it. No, I don't like it at all! I don't agree!"

He was silent, but soon broke out again.

"No, I'm not the sort to hold out my neck to Charon like a sheep and say: 'Cut my throat, Mr. Charon, please: I want to go straight to Paradise!' "

I listened to Zorba in perplexity. Who was the sage who tried to teach his disciples to do voluntarily what the law ordered should be done? To say "yes" to necessity and change the inevitable into something done of their own free will? That is perhaps the only human way to deliverance. It is a pitiable way, but there is no other.

But what of revolt? The proud, quixotic reaction of mankind to conquer Necessity and make external laws conform to the internal laws of the soul, to deny all that is and create a new world according to the laws of one's own heart, which are contrary to the inhuman laws of nature—to create a new world which is purer, better and more moral than the one that exists?

Zorba looked at me, saw that I had no more to say to him, took up the cage carefully so that he should not wake the parrot, placed it by his head and stretched out on the pebbles.

"Good night, boss!" he said. "That's enough."

A strong south wind was blowing from Africa. It was making the vegetables and fruits and Cretan breasts all swell and grow. I felt it on my forehead, lips and neck; and like a fruit my brain cracked and swelled.

I could not and would not sleep. I thought of nothing. I just felt something, someone growing to maturity inside me in the warm night. I lived lucidly through a most surprising experience: I saw myself change. A thing that usually happens only in the most obscure depths of our bowels was this time occurring in the open, before my eyes. Crouched by the sea, I watched this miracle take place.

The stars grew dim, the sky grew light and against this luminous background appeared, as if delicately traced in ink, the mountains, trees and gulls.

Dawn was breaking.

from The Stranger

Albert Camus

Meursault, the hero of Camus' penetrating existential novel, is sentenced to death for a murder. His guilt is unimportant at this point. In too many ways, Meursault is being executed for his failure to react, act, feel, think, and grieve in precisely the same fashion as his fellows. His judges remember back to the funeral of his own mother, when he could not, or would not, weep. Perhaps it is this "image" of Meursault that is tried, judged, and convicted.

In this excerpt, Meursault is spending his last night in the cell. At dawn, he will die. He rejects the usual social amenities. This, of course, increases his captors' conviction that he is a cold-blooded villain. Read his words and decide for yourself.

Then all day there was my appeal to think about. I made the most of this idea, studying my effects so as to squeeze out the maximum of consolation. Thus, I always began by assuming the worst; my appeal was dismissed. That meant, of course, I was to die. Sooner than others, obviously. "But," I reminded myself, "it's common knowledge that life isn't worth living, anyhow." And, on a wide view, I could see that it makes little difference whether one dies at the age of thirty or threescore and ten—since, in either case, other men and women will continue living, the world will go on as before. Also, whether I died now or forty years hence, this business of dying had to be got through, inevitably. Still, somehow this line of thought wasn't as consoling as it should have been; the idea of all those years of life in hand was a galling reminder! However, I could argue myself out of it, by picturing what would have been my feelings when my term was up, and death had cornered me. Once you're up against it, the precise manner of your death has obviously small importance. Therefore—but it was hard not to lose the thread of the argument leading up to that "therefore"—I should be prepared to face the dismissal of my appeal.

At this stage, but only at this stage, I had, so to speak, the *right,* and accordingly I gave myself leave, to consider the other alternative; that my appeal was successful. And then the trouble was to calm down that sudden rush of joy racing through my body and even bringing tears to my eyes. But it was up to me to bring my nerves to heel and steady my mind; for, even in considering this possibility, I had to keep some order in my thoughts, so as to make my consolations, as regards the first alternative, more plausible. When I'd succeeded, I had earned a good hour's peace of mind; and that, anyhow, was something.

It was at one of these moments that I refused once again to see the chaplain. I was lying down and could mark the summer evening coming on by a soft golden glow spreading across the sky. I had just turned down my appeal, and felt my blood circulating with slow, steady throbs. No, I didn't want to see the chaplain. . . . Then I did something I hadn't done for quite a while; I fell to thinking about Marie. She hadn't written for ages; probably, I surmised, she had grown tired of being the mistress of a man sentenced to death. Or she might be ill, or dead. After all, such things happen. How could I have known about it, since, apart from our two bodies, separated now, there was no link between us, nothing to remind us of each other? Supposing she were dead, her memory would mean nothing; I couldn't feel an interest in a dead girl. This seemed to me quite normal; just as I realized people would soon forget me once I was dead. I couldn't even say that this was hard to stomach; really, there's no idea to which one doesn't get acclimatized in time.

My thoughts had reached this point when the chaplain walked in, unannounced. I couldn't help giving a start on seeing him. He noticed this evidently, as he promptly told me not to be alarmed. I reminded him that usually his visits were at another hour, and for a pretty grim occasion. This, he replied, was just a friendly visit; it had no concern with my appeal, about which he knew nothing. Then he sat down on my bed, asking me to sit beside him. I refused—not because I had anything against him; he seemed a mild, amiable man.

He remained quite still at first, his arms resting on his knees, his eyes fixed on his hands. They were slender but sinewy hands, which made me think of two nimble little animals. Then he gently rubbed them together. He stayed so long in the same position that for a while I almost forgot he was there.

All of a sudden he jerked his head up and looked me in the eyes. "Why," he asked, "don't you let me come to see you?"

I explained that I didn't believe in God.

"Are you really so sure of that?"

I said I saw no point in troubling my head about the matter; whether I believed or didn't was, to my mind, a question of so little importance.

He then leaned back against the wall, laying his hands flat on his thighs. Almost without seeming to address me, he remarked that he'd often noticed one fancies one is quite sure about something, when in point of fact, one isn't. When I said nothing, he looked at me again, and asked:

"Don't you agree?"

I said that seemed quite possible. But, though I mightn't be so sure about what interested me, I was absolutely sure about what didn't interest me. And the question he had raised didn't interest me at all.

He looked away and, without altering his posture, asked if it was because I felt utterly desperate that I spoke like this. I explained that it wasn't despair I felt, but fear—which was natural enough.

"In that case," he said firmly, "God can help you. All the men I've seen in your position turned to Him in their time of trouble."

Obviously, I replied, they were at liberty to do so, if they felt like it. I, however, didn't want to be helped, and I hadn't time to work up interest for something that didn't interest me.

He fluttered his hands fretfully; then, sitting up, smoothed out his cassock. When this was done he began talking again, addressing me as "my friend." It wasn't because I'd been condemned to death, he said, that he spoke to me in this way. In his opinion every man on the earth was under sentence of death.

There, I interrupted him; that wasn't the same thing, I pointed out, and, what's more, could be no consolation.

He nodded. "Maybe. Still, if you don't die soon, you'll die one day. And then the same question will arise. How will you face that terrible, final hour?"

I replied that I'd face it exactly as I was facing it now.

Thereat he stood up, and looked me straight in the eyes. It was a trick I knew well. I used to amuse myself trying it on Emmanuel and Celeste, and nine times out of ten they'd look away uncomfortably. I could see the chaplain was an old hand at it, as his gaze never faltered. And his voice was quite steady when he said: "Have you no hope at all? Do you really think that when you die you die outright, and nothing remains?"

I said: "Yes."

He dropped his eyes and sat down again. He was truly sorry for me, he said. It must make life unbearable for a man, to think as I did.

The priest was beginning to bore me, and, resting a shoulder on the wall, just beneath the little skylight, I looked away. Though I didn't trouble much to follow what he said, I gathered he was questioning me again. Presently, his tone became agitated, urgent, and as I realized that he was genuinely distressed, I began to pay more attention.

He said he felt convinced my appeal would succeed, but I was saddled with a load of guilt, of which I must get rid. In his view man's justice was a vain thing; only God's justice mattered. I pointed out that the former had condemned me. Yes, he agreed, but it hadn't absolved me from my sin. I told him that I wasn't conscious of any "sin"; all I knew was that I'd been guilty of a criminal offense. Well, I was paying the penalty of that offense, and no one had the right to expect anything more of me.

Just then he got up again, and it struck me that if he wanted to move in this tiny cell, almost the only choice lay between standing up and sitting down. I was staring at the floor. He took a single step toward me, and halted, as if he didn't dare to come nearer. Then he looked up through the bars at the sky.

"You're mistaken, my son," he said gravely. "There's more that might be required of you. And perhaps it *will* be required of you."

"What do you mean?"

"You might be asked to see . . ."

"To see what?"

Slowly the priest gazed round my cell, and I was struck by the sadness of his voice when he replied:

"These stone walls, I know it only too well, are steeped in human suffering. I've never been able to look at them without a shudder. And yet—believe me, I am speaking from the depths of my heart—I *know* that even the wretchedest amongst you have sometimes seen, taking form against that grayness, a divine face. It's that face you are asked to see."

This roused me a little. I informed him that I'd been staring at those walls for months; there was nobody, nothing in the world, I knew better than I knew them. And once upon a time, perhaps, I used to try to see a face. But it was a sun-gold face, lit up with desire—Marie's face. I had no luck; I'd never seen it, and now I'd given up trying. Indeed, I'd never seen anything "taking form" as he called it, against those gray walls.

The chaplain gazed at me with a sort of sadness. I now had my back to the wall and light was flowing over my forehead. He muttered some words I didn't catch; then abruptly asked if he might kiss me. I said, "No." Then he turned, came up to the wall, and slowly drew his hand along it.

"Do you really love these earthly things so very much?" he asked in a low voice.

I made no reply.

For quite a while he kept his eyes averted. His presence was getting more and more irksome, and I was on the point of telling him to go, and leave me in peace, when all of a sudden he swung round on me, and burst out passionately:

"No! No! I refuse to believe it. I'm sure you've often wished there was an afterlife."

Of course I had, I told him. Everybody has that wish at times. But that had no more importance than wishing to be rich, or to swim very fast, or to have a better-shaped mouth. It was in the same vein, when he cut in with a question. How did I picture the life after the grave?

I fairly bawled out at him: "A life in which I can remember this life on earth. That's all I want of it." And in the same breath I told him I'd had enough of his company.

But, apparently, he had more to say on the subject of God. I went close up to him and made a last attempt to explain that I'd very little time left, and I wasn't going to waste it on God.

Then he tried to change the subject by asking me why I hadn't once addressed him as "Father," seeing that he was a priest. That irritated me still more, and I told him he wasn't my father; quite the contrary, he was on the others' side.

"No, no, my son," he said, laying his hand on my shoulder, "I'm on *your* side, though you don't realize it—because your heart is hardened. But I shall pray for you."

Then, I don't know how it was, but something seemed to break inside me, and I started yelling at the top of my voice. I hurled insults at him, I told him not to waste his rotten prayers on me; it was better to burn than to disappear. I'd taken him by the neckband of his cassock, and, in a sort of ecstasy of joy and rage, I poured out on him all the thoughts that had been simmering in my brain. He seemed so cocksure, you see. And yet none of his certainties was worth one strand of a woman's hair. Living as he did, like a corpse, he couldn't even be sure of being alive. It might look as if my hands were empty. Actually I was sure of myself, sure about everything, far surer than he; sure of my present life and of the death that was coming. That, no doubt, was all I had; but at least that certainty was something I could get my teeth into—just as it had got its teeth into me. I'd been right, I was still right, I was always right. I'd passed my life in a certain way, and I might have passed it in a different way, and I might have passed it in a different way, if I'd felt like it. I'd acted thus, and I hadn't acted otherwise; I hadn't done *x,* whereas I had done *y* or *z.* And what did that mean? That, all the time, I'd been waiting for this present moment, for that dawn, tomorrow's or another day's, which was to justify me. Nothing, nothing had the least importance, and I knew quite well why. He, too, knew why. From the dark horizon of my future a sort of slow, persistent breeze had been blowing toward me, all my life long, from the years that were to come. And on its way that breeze had leveled out all the ideas that people tried to foist on me in the equally unreal years I then was living through. What difference could they make to me, the deaths of others, or a mother's love, or his God; or the way a man decides to live, the fate he thinks he chooses, since one and the same fate was bound to "choose" not only me but thousands of millions of privileged people who, like him, called themselves my brothers. Surely, surely he must see that? Every man alive was privileged; there was only one class of men, the privileged class. All alike would be condemned to die one day; his turn, too, would come like the others'. And what difference could it make if, after being charged with murder, he were executed because he didn't weep at his mother's funeral, since it all came to the same thing in the end? . . .

... Almost for the first time in many months I thought of my mother. And now, it seemed to me, I understand why at her life's end she had taken on a "fiancé"; why she'd played at making a fresh start. There, too, in that Home where lives were flickering out, the dusk came as a mournful solace. With death so near, Mother must have felt like someone on the brink of freedom, ready to start life all over again. No one, no one in the world had any right to weep for her. And I, too, felt ready to start life all over again. It was as if that great rush of anger had washed me clean, emptied me of hope, and, gazing up at the dark sky spangled with its signs and stars, for the first time, the first, I laid my heart open to the benign indifference of the universe. To feel it so like myself, indeed, so brotherly, made me realize that I'd been happy, and that I was happy still.

The Nature of Man

What is man? This is the age-old question. The Psalmist asked it of his God, wondering how the deity could pay so much attention to such an insignificant part of the universe. Shakespeare extolled man throughout his poetic career, but colored his entire catalog of works with a touch of irony that betrayed his curiosity and bemusement at this "piece of work."

This is essentially a philosophical problem, and psychologists are discovering that they cannot do a good job of understanding human nature without coming to grips with this philosophical question. Since we agree that "the proper study of mankind is man," we turn to those who have a sympathetic but reality-oriented approach to the matter.

Hadley Cantril is a psychologist who has spent many years researching a variety of subjects. He has pioneered in the study of perception, the processes by which we make sense out of our sense experiences. In *A Fresh Look at the Human Design* he tries to point out that human motivation—what makes us tick—is much more complicated than we've been told by people who work with rats and guinea pigs.

The nature of man question brings us squarely to the fact of our interpersonal dimensions and relations. Are we only animals, only souls, only brains? Does the way we view our own nature have anything to say about the way in which we relate to each other?

Dr. Everett Shostrom, a psychologist in practice in his own psychotherapeutic institute in California, combines the insights of Abraham Maslow, Eric Berne, and the Gestalt Therapy of Fritz Perls in his explorations of human behavior. In this excerpt from *Man, The Manipulator,* we get insight into some of the different ways in which we can relate to each other.

A Fresh Look at the Human Design

Hadley Cantril

Man, as Dr. James Bugental tells us, is the challenge to man. But most of our studies of human experience are dull and uninteresting because the student can't find himself in the literature. He reads about the "organism" or the "subject," but fails to find the flesh and blood being that he can identify with. Cantril tells us that we are far more than a combination of stimulus-response patterns. In this excerpt, he tells us of the complex matter of human nature in terms of the things that really motivate people.

The human being seems at last to be entering the main body of psychology with a vengeance. For years he has all too often been shorn of his most characteristic attributes, until he has been scarcely recognizable. Variables such as appetites, wants, values, and temperament have been neglected because they are not easily manipulated in the laboratory and can so disturb otherwise neat experimentation. As Henry A. Murray pointed out nearly two decades ago (1948, p. 466), "The main body of psychology started its career by putting the wrong foot forward, and it

Excerpted from *The Challenges of Humanistic Psychology,* James F. T. Bugental, ed. (New York: Mc-Graw-Hill Book Company, 1967), pp. 13–18.

has been out of step with the march of science much of the time. Instead of beginning with studies of the whole person adjusting to a natural environment, it began with studies of a segment of a person responding to a physical stimulus in an unnatural laboratory environment." One consequence of this false start has been a proliferation of model building which often takes on the aspect of playing games. Another consequence has been an overemphasis by some investigators on a single variable which proves at best tentative and partial after the fad for it has run its course.

It is therefore no wonder that so many students of psychology have found it an insufferably dull subject and that many social scientists and inquiring laymen feel that most of the psychology they read provides them unconvincing, unrewarding concepts from which to choose as they try to give plausible accounts of the behavior of men and women in real-life situations. They sense that somewhere along the line too much of human experience has been left out of account.

It is appropriate, then, for those of us concerned with human experience and behavior in all its subtle ramifications to spell out what seems to us to ring true and what appear to be the demands that the genetically built-in design of the human being imposes on any society, political culture, or enduring social relationship. It is all too easy to neglect the basic functional uniformities which take diverse forms and to leave the accounting or explanation at that level. Differences are often dramatic and simpler to detect than the similarities they may obscure. Here I shall try to orchestrate into some systematic unity the diversities of mankind found in different societies and contexts. . . .

Man Requires the Satisfaction of His Survival Needs

Any listing of the characteristics of any living organism must begin here. Neurophysiologists have located and described in a most general way two built-in appetitive systems found in higher animals: one system propelling them to seek satisfying and pleasurable experiences, and the other protecting them from threatening or unpleasant experiences (Cantril & Livingston, 1963). These two systems together can be thought of as the basic forces contained within all human beings, which not only keep them and the species alive as their simple survival needs for food, shelter, and sex are gratified but also are involved in the desire for life itself.

These appetitive systems, of course, become enormously developed, refined, and conditioned—especially in man—as new ways are learned to achieve satisfactions and avoid dangers and discomforts. It has often been noted that unless the survival needs are satisfied, a person devotes himself almost exclusively to a continued attempt to fulfill them, a preoccupation which preempts his energies and repels any concern for other activities. Most people in the world today are still concerned with living a type of life that constitutes well-being on a relatively simple level with what amenities their cultures can provide.

Man Wants Security in Both Its Physical and Its Psychological Meaning to Protect Gains Already Made and to Assure a Beachhead from Which Further Advances May be Staged

Man wants some surety that one action can lead to another, some definite foothold which provides an orientation and integration through time. People invariably become embittered if they nurse a dream for what they regard as a long time with no signs of it becoming a reality. . . .

Man Craves Sufficient Order and Certainty in His Life to Enable Him to Judge with Fair Accuracy What Will or Will Not Occur if He Does or Does Not Act in Certain Ways

People want sufficient form and pattern in life to be sure that certain satisfactions already enjoyed will be repeatable and will provide a secure springboard for takeoffs in new directions.

The conflict of old loyalties with emerging new loyalties in the case of developing people is bound to create uncertainties, doubts and hesitations. If people become frustrated and anxious enough, they will do almost anything in a desperate attempt to put some order into apparent chaos or rally around new symbols and abstractions that enable them to identify with a new order that promises to alleviate the uncertainties experienced in the here and now.

In stressing process and change, the desire of people to preserve the *status quo* when it has proved satisfying and rewarding and to protect existing forms against alteration must never be overlooked. This craving for certainty would include the satisfactions that come from the sense of stability provided by our habitual behavior—including much of our social and political behavior.

Human Beings Continuously Seek to Enlarge the Range and Enrich the Quality of Their Satisfactions.

Man is engaged in a ceaseless quest to extend the range and improve the quality of his satisfactions through the exercise of his creative and inventive capacities. This is, of course, a basic reason why order of any kind is constantly being upset. Whitehead expressed the point eloquently and repeatedly, for example, in his statements that "the essence of life is to be found in the frustrations of established order" (1938, p. 119) and that "the art of progress is to preserve order amid change, and to preserve change amid order" (1929, p. 515).

The distinguished British philosopher John Macmurray has used the phrase "the self as agent" as the title of his book analyzing the role of action in man's constant search for value satisfactions (1957). In a companion volume, he has noted that ". . . human behavior cannot be understood, but only caricatured, if it is represented as an adaptation to environment" (1961, p. 46). The search for an enlargement of satisfactions in the transactions of living can also be phrased as the *desire for development in a direction,* the desire to do something which will bring a sense of accomplishment as we experience the consequences of successfully carrying out some intention and which will thus give us an occasional feeling that our lives are continuous creations in which we can take an active part. During a conversation in Beirut, a wise man once remarked to me that "people are hungry for new and good experiences.". . .

The particular value satisfactions man acquires are the result of learning. Some of the values learned will serve as the operative ideals of a people; others will be chiefly instrumental. People in rich countries have learned to want and to expect many aspects of a good life that less favored people have not yet learned are possibilities. From this point of view, one might say that the competition between social and political systems is a competition in teaching people what to want and what is potentially available to them, and then in proving to them in their own private experience that these wants are best attainable under the system described.

Human Beings Are Creatures of Hope and Are Not Genetically Designed to Resign Themselves

This characteristic of man stems from the characteristic just described: that man is always likely to be dissatisfied and never fully "adapts" to his environment.

Man seems continually to hope that the world he encounters will correspond more and more to his vision of it as he acts within it to carry out his purposes, while the vision itself continuously unfolds in an irreversible direction. The whole process is a never-ending one. It is characteristic of man in his ongoing experience to ask himself, "Where do I go from here?" Only in his more reflective moods does a person ask, "Where did I come from?" or "How did I get this way?" Most of the time, most people who are "plugged into" the changing world around them are future-oriented in their concerns.

Human Beings Have the Capacity to Make Choices and the Desire to Exercise This Capacity

Any mechanical model of man, constructed by a psychologist or by anyone else is bound to leave out the crucially important characteristic of man as an "appetitive-perceptive agency." Perceptions are learned and utilized by people to provide prognoses or bets of a variety of kinds to weigh alternative courses of action to achieve purposes. Consciously or without conscious awareness, people are trying to perceive the probable relation between their potential acts and the consequences of these acts to the intentions that constitute their goals.

The human nervous system, including the brain, has the capacity to police its input, to determine what is and what is not significant for it, and to pay attention to and to reinforce or otherwise modify its behavior as it transacts in the occasions of living (Cantril & Livingston, 1963). In this sense, the human being is a participant in, and producer of, his own value satisfactions: People perceive only what is relevant to their purposes and make their choices accordingly.

Human Beings Require Freedom to Exercise the Choices They Are Capable of Making

This characteristic of man related to freedom is deliberately worded as it is, rather than as a blanket statement that "human beings require freedom," since the freedom people want is so relative to their desires and the stage of development they have attained. Human beings, incidentally, apparently require more freedom than other species of animals because of their much greater capacity to move about and to engage in a much wider variety of behavior.

It seems true that maximum freedom is a necessary condition if a highly developed individual is to obtain maximum value satisfaction. It is equally true, as many people have pointed out, that too much freedom too soon can be an unbearable burden and a source of bondage if people, like children, are insufficiently developed to know what to do with it. For freedom clearly involves a learning of responsibility and an ability to take advantage of it wisely.

The concept of freedom is essentially a psychological and not a political concept. It describes an individual's opportunity to make his own choices and to act in accord with them. Psychologically, freedom refers to the freedom to experience more of what is potentially available, the freedom to move about and ahead, to be and to become. Freedom is thus less and less determined and more of a reality as man evolves and develops; it emerges and flowers as people learn what it can mean to them in terms of resolving some frustrations under which they are living. . . .

Human Beings Want to Experience Their Own Identity and Integrity

(More Popularly Referred to as the "Need for Personal Dignity.") Every human being craves a sense of his own self-constancy, an assurance of the repeatability of experience in which he is a determining participant. He obtains this from the transactions he has with other individuals.

People develop significances they share with others in their membership and reference groups. If the satisfaction derived from and the significance of participation with others cease to confirm assumptions or to enrich values, then a person's sense of self-constancy becomes shaken or insecure, and his loyalties become formalized and empty or are given up altogether. He becomes alienated or seeks new significances, new loyalties that are more operationally real.

People Want to Experience a Sense of Their Own Worthwhileness

This differentiation is made from the desire for personal identity and integrity to bring out the important relationship between this search for identity and the behavior and attitudes of others toward us. A human being wants to know he is valued by others and that others will somehow show through their behavior that his own behavior and its consequences make some sort of difference to them in ways that give him a sense of satisfaction. When this occurs, not only is a person's sense of identity confirmed, but he also experiences a sense of personal worth and self-respect. The process of extending the sense of self both in space and in time appears also to involve the desire that one's "presence" not be limited merely to the here and now of existence, but extend into larger dimensions. These human cravings seem to be at the root of man's social relationships.

People acquire, maintain, and enrich their sense of worthwhileness only if they at least vaguely recognize the sources of what personal identity they have: their family, their friends and neighbors, their associates or fellow workers, their group ties, or their nation. The social, religious, intellectual, regional, or national loyalties formed play the important role of making it possible for individuals to extend themselves backward into the past and forward into the future and to identify themselves with others who live at more or less remote distances from them. This means the compounding of shared experiences into a bundle that can be conceptualized, felt, or somehow referred to in the here and now of daily living, thus making a person feel a functional part of a more enduring alliance. Man accomplishes such feats of self-extension largely through his capacity to create symbols, images, and myths which provide focal points for identification and self-expansion. After reviewing the lessons from history, Muller noted as one of the "forgotten simplicities" the fact that "men have always been willing to sacrifice themselves for some larger cause, fighting and dying for their family, tribe, or community, with or without hope of eternal reward" (1954, p. 392).

Human Beings Seek Some Value or System of Beliefs to Which They Can Commit Themselves

In the midst of the probabilities and uncertainties that surround them, people want some anchoring points, some certainties, some faith that will serve either as a beacon light to guide them or as a balm to assuage them during the inevitable frustrations and anxieties that living engenders.

People who have long been frustrated and who have searched for means to alleviate their situations are, of course, particularly susceptible to a commitment to a new system of beliefs or an ideology that they feel holds promise of effective action.

Beliefs are confirmed insofar as action based on them brings satisfying consequences, and they are denied with growing skepticism if disastrous results consistently occur because they are followed.

Commitment to a value or belief system becomes more difficult among well-informed and sophisticated people who self-consciously try to reconcile what they believe with what they know and what they know with what they believe. In such circumstances, beliefs become more secular and less important as personal identifications.

Human Beings Want a Sense of Surety and Confidence that the Society of Which They Are a Part Holds out a Fair Degree of Hope that Their Aspirations Will be Fulfilled

If people cannot experience the effectiveness of social mechanisms to accomplish some of the potential goals they aspire to, then obviously their frustrations and anxieties mount, and they search for new means to accomplish aims. On the other hand, they make any sacrifice required to protect a society which they feel is fulfilling their needs but which appears seriously threatened. . . .

. . . If the gap between what society actually provides in terms of effective mechanisms for living and what it purports to provide becomes too great, the vacuum created will sooner or later engender the frustrations that urge people on to seek new social patterns and symbols. Whitehead wrote (1927, p. 88):

> The major advances in civilization are processes which all but wreck the societies in which they occur—like unto an arrow in the hand of a child. The art of free society consists first in the maintenance of the symbolic code; and secondly in fearlessness of revision, to secure that the code serves those purposes which satisfy an enlightened reason. Those societies which cannot combine reverence to their symbols with freedom of revision, must ultimately decay either from anarchy, or from the slow atrophy of a life stifled by useless shadows.

Every social and political system can be regarded as an experiment in the broad perspective of time. Whatever the experiment, the human design will in the long run force any experiment to accommodate to it. This has been the case throughout human history. Few would deny that the varied patterns of experiments going on today hold out more promise of satisfying the human condition for a greater number of people than ever before.

REFERENCES

Cantril, H., & Livington, W. K. The Concept of Transaction in Psychology and Neurology. *Journal of Individual Psychology,* 1963, 19, 3—16.

Macmurray, J. *The Self as Agent.* New York: Harper & Row, 1957.

Macmurray, J. *Persons in Relation.* London: Faber, 1961.

Muller, H. J. *The Uses of the Past.* New York: Mentor Books, 1954.

Murray, H. A., et al. *The Assessment of Men.* New York: Holt, Rinehart and Winston, 1948.

Whitehead, A. N. *Symbolism: Its Meaning and Effect.* New York: Macmillan, 1929.

Whitehead, A. N. *Modes of Thought.* New York: Macmillan, 1938.

Profit *vs.* Persons

Everett Shostrom

In his exciting best-seller, *Man, The Manipulator,* Dr. Everett Shostrom tries to differentiate between those of us who play the games needed to manipulate, exploit, abuse, and control other people from those who try to actualize their latent potentials.

In this short excerpt, Dr. Shostrom describes the philosophical orientations of people in our society that make many people move away from self-actualization and into the somewhat safer, but far less satisfying, arena of manipulation-playing.

I notice all through these pages that my case histories show businessmen coming to me for help in their personal lives. The paradox is that they are very successful men, according to their profit and loss statements, yet seem to be most unsuccessful measured by the quality of their interpersonal relationships. They can't seem to avoid problems with their wives or their children or their friends. Obviously the question arises: is the underlying philosophy of business a breeder of manipulators?

This has to concern us because the most potent single institution in our American culture is business and industry, and there are some critics who suggest that many American industrial leaders have used manipulation to achieve their goals. As we have seen . . . , manipulation in *personal* relations is dangerous and self-defeating. But maybe the rules for business and personal life are different? In business a person has to make a profit, and that might seem to require manipulation.

In an area as big and complex as this, I do not pretend to give hard-and-fast answers. I go back instead to the basic principle on which the book is based. You will remember that I referred to the manipulative relationship as an "it-it" relationship in which the person who regards another as an "it" or a "thing" also becomes an "it" or "thing." A businessman who thinks of people only as customers or accounts or clients cannot help, to some degree, regarding these persons as things. When profit is the primary concern, then, it seems to me from my own experience that it is easy to lose one's sensitivity to the personhood of another.

Earlier, I proposed that the model for an actualizing relationship is a "thou-thou" relationship, where the person who regards another as a "thou" also becomes a "thou." In my work as therapist, this is easy for me to do since therapy is based on respect for the dignity and worth of one's client. But the fact that he *is* a client, and not just a person, makes him also a matter of financial concern to me. When I am being the businessman, rather than the psychologist, it is difficult not to let the "thou" become a "thing."

Perhaps people don't think of the psychologist in terms of his being also a businessman. Make no mistake about it, though, I must be a businessman and must, therefore, have this great general conflict in myself. At the Institute, for instance, I have a sizeable overhead to be met every month before I can start earning a livelihood for my family. I must charge a fee for my services and must collect my accounts. An electric typewriter costs me just as much as it does General Motors. I have gas bills, electrical bills, a huge telephone bill, and must buy malpractice insurance the same as doctors and lawyers. I pay six cents to mail a letter or the bill for my services just as the businessman down the street does. I must pay Social Security and withholding taxes on the skilled secretaries who have typed these words. The conflict between the businessman side of me and the therapist side of me is ever present.

I would like to propose that there is an interesting parallel between my work as psychologist and that of the businessman. To the therapist, the patient is relatively the same as the employee or customer is to the businessman; the patient who comes to the Institute is both a person to be helped and a client to be served. To the businessman, although he may not always remember it, his customer and employees are as much persons as are his wife and children.

The basic problem of the patient is that he uses "crutches" when he doesn't need them. He tries constantly to manipulate the therapist for support, and my job is to frustrate him in his demands so he can stop manipulating and become self-actualizing—so he can trust himself rather than depend on me or other people. The less internal support he has, the more he has to manipulate.

A parallel situation exists between employee and employer. The employee is a person who depends on his employer for economic support. In an age of fringe benefits it is only natural that he will try to get as many as he can for as little work as possible. In this he is like the patient trying to get as much support from the psychologist as the traffic will bear. An actualizing employer would be the one who helps his employee become increasingly self-supporting, in the sense that he learns to do the job better. But then, ironically, the employee may want more of the profit or more rewards for doing his job better, and the facts of good business practice are that there is a limit to how much you can pay him. We are seeing the ultimate tragedy of this on all sides of our modern society, in the growth of automation. Here the employer, of necessity, is learning to make things—machines—replace people.

There is another parallel. A patient sometimes demands excessive attention at all hours of the day or night, whenever he is in trouble and thinks I should help; he also feels entitled to run up as large a bill as he needs. Some even expect me to see them for nothing if they are unable to pay, manipulating me into thinking I am a public servant who cannot deny the needy. The answer to them must be: My love is free, but you must pay for my time. I will continue to regard the individual as a "thou," but my time is limited, and I must be recompensed for it.

The businessman has a similar implied philosophy toward his customers. His attitude, for instance: You expect of me certain services; you expect conveniences from my place of business, savings, quality, personal attention. The bargain-conscious customer, on his part, demands that the businessman charge less than his competition. (As witness to this, we have the current mushroom growth of discount houses.) The facts of economic life are that the merchant expects to provide products as cheaply as it can be done but expects also that you, the customer, pay for the services rendered.

At this point advertising complicates the problem. In order to attract the customer to a given merchant or product, advertising attempts to portray that store or that commodity as the best or the cheapest, whether it always is true or not. Advertising costs money, of course, and that must be added to the price of the product. Consider the phenomenon of trading stamps. We are led to assume that the stamps are given to us free with our purchases and that we obtain expensive articles for them gratis. In reality, of course, we pay for these bonus items because they have been paid for by the retailer, who has added the expense of the stamps to the cost of the product he sold us in the first place. We allow ourselves to be manipulated in this stamp dealing, pleasant though it may seem.

Selling intrudes a further complication in this matter of profit versus persons. To sell we must have salesmen, and again it is Abraham Maslow who offers us some thinking.[1] The typical salesman is profit motivated. He knows he must curry favor with the customer by building his loyalty; therefore, the salesman is prepared to spend substantial amounts of expense money entertaining customers and cementing their friendship to induce purchasing. He is the manipulator par excellence. I have, as a matter of fact, had a number of salesmen as patients who had to give up the work because they were becoming ill from having to play phoney friendship games with people they didn't really like. The usual salesman, as we would expect, is a profit-oriented man, loyal to his company and product, who functions partially on a selective presentation of information and truth. The main goal of his business dealings is to market the product (even though it may be inferior) since the success of his company depends on it.

---

1. See Abraham H. Maslow, *Eupsychian Management* (Homewood, Ill.: Richard D. Irwin, 1965).

Maslow suggests an alternative. He suggests that businessmen try to assume that the good customer is a rational human being who prefers quality in merchandising, that he has taste and is capable of righteous indignation. This customer realizes that expense account lunches and phoney friendship weekends are actually costs which will only be added to the price of the product. Maslow proposes then that the salesman re-identify himself as a man of integrity who knows his product and the market, sees himself as an "ambassador" in the business world, relying upon honesty, truthfulness, and full disclosure of the facts. To this type of salesman, *marketing of the product would be secondary to the interests and needs of the customer.* This might even mean recommending another company's product if the salesman truly feels that product would better meet the needs of this customer. I'm sure this will all sound ridiculously idealistic to some salesmen, advertising executives, and executive suite top dogs. The fact is, however, that there are companies who are succeeding on the basis of this very philosophy.

None of us wants to be treated like a child so stupid he cannot see the transparency of high-pressure retailing practices. Although we may continue to buy the products, most of us are moved to scoff at the techniques, for instance, by which cigarettes are sold by associating smoking with sexual charm or masculinity. I actually marvel at the way in which soap manufacturers have convinced us that we smell so badly! Keeping in sight of our concern with manipulations, note how even guilt is used as a motivating technique in merchandising: selling insurance by making the customer feel guilty unless he provides well for his children; selling tires by making the customer feel guilty unless he provides for the safety of his family; selling photographs by making the customer feel guilty unless he provides each child with a memory photograph album. I am not passing moral judgment on this since I am not sure I know what the alternatives are—in the business ethics of my own profession, I am not permitted to advertise—but I'm sure we all recognize what seedbeds exist in this environment for manipulation.

Businessmen patients and friends constantly raise the fundamental issue of how to succeed in business without really manipulating. As yet, I confess, I haven't been able to answer them very well. Is it possible that there can be a "good manipulation" in business, where a supposedly more mature person chooses for, and controls the decision of, the more immature? Can a "Thou" (spelled with a capital "T") ever decide for a "thou" (spelled with a small "t") without making him an "it" or a "thing"? Certainly such a decision would not be actualizing because the theory of actualizing is to help the more immature individual become more mature. This he cannot do if he is kept in a state of stupidity and dependence.

I realize that this all gets pretty close to the heart of our capitalistic system—it would seem to indicate that this aspect of the system needs a thorough re-examination—but, before someone accuses me of being against our free enterprise system, which I am not, let me quote the late Adlai Stevenson: "The real patriots are those who love America as she is, but who want the beloved to be more lovable. This is not treachery. This, as every parent, every teacher, every friend must know, is the truest and noblest affection."[2] I love America above all other countries and ways of life. Nevertheless, I am concerned with how we can do business and yet return to our original concepts of the worth and dignity of man.

Clergymen of all faiths have wrestled with the problem for years. Businessmen are not ipso facto soulless individuals; without their sincere and open-handed support, we could not have the magnificent church structure that is a part of our way of life. Still there is the conflict, which the great psychoanalyst, Karen Horney, has posed very clearly. The contradiction, she says, is one of valuing the concept of competition in the American way of life on the one hand, and of brotherly love and humility on the other. On the one hand, we are supposed to be assertive and aggressive and push all competitors out of the way. On the other hand, clergymen tell us not to be selfish, that we should be humble, turn the other cheek, and love our neighbor rather than compete with him. The modern manipulator feels this contradiction deeply.

Psychologists and psychiatrists are called upon daily to help unravel the tangled patterns manipulating businessmen weave into their lives. The goal of our therapy is to help them find their own creative synthesis of the polarities that they all possess. As I have stated often in this book, the ultimate objective is to become the many-splendored person of complementary opposites—the person who has found his creative synthesis. As an answer to Karen Horney's dilemma, I would suggest

---

2. P. Steiner, *The Stevenson Wit and Wisdom* (New York: Pyramid Books, 1965), p. 130.

that the aggressive manipulator, as well as the over-sympathetic lover, can find an actualizing, creative synthesis when he becomes "assertively caring." This, of course, requires a process of therapy and is not done simply by willing it.

While the overall question remains unanswered, and I confess my inadequacy to come up with a satisfactory answer as yet, my telephone continues to ring. My therapy room continues to fill up with troubled persons. For those whose manipulative habits in business have brought them to my door, I can at least offer Kant's extraordinary creative suggestion: Be yourself; find your creative ethic within (as this book has been proposing). However, let it be possible that your inner ethic is capable of serving as a norm for mankind as a whole! To the individual businessman who has gotten into difficulty through manipulations and whose health and survival seem to demand it, I recommend that he consider the actualizing alternative, even though it may mean he will be less successful in the marketplace. As we read in Matthew 16:26, *For what is a man profited, if he shall gain the whole world, and lose his own soul?*

The Biosocial Experience

Man is more than an animal, but he *is* an animal. This is the paradox and the source of much of our confusion about human nature. Those who make of man nothing more than a bundle of reflexes, instincts, and sensations do human nature a disservice. Other people, who make man a deity or a disembodied spirit, ignore the very real evidence of man's physical nature.

The complexity of man's nature, in addition to confusing our simplistic schemes, also provides us with rich ground for research and exploration. Man is neither ape nor angel. Man is man. He is part of the animal kingdom, but responds differently than any other animal to various kinds of situations and stimuli. He is a creator of stimulation as well as an organism that responds to it. In addition, man is social. He is born into social groupings and never ceases to have some involvement with other people.

William Schutz is a psychologist in California. His work in sensitivity training and psychotherapy has convinced him that man needs to get back into touch with his own physical, biological nature. In the excerpt from his best-selling book, *Joy: Expanding Human Awareness,* Dr. Schutz describes the importance of recovering our own physical awareness, which is an important part of his sensitivity and therapeutic work.

The second selection is a short story by Robert G. Amick, one of the editors of this anthology, entitled *Optimal Jones and His Wife Belle*. Amick attempts to explore the interaction of man, his society, and his physical environment in some "ideal world" of the future, when most of the problems we now consider to be the most pressing will have been solved.

excerpt from *Joy*

William C. Schutz

Joy is a three-letter word to most of us. To Dr. William Schutz it's the by-product of real and full self-discovery. It comes not so much through the usual means of joy-production that most of us use: alcohol, sex, drugs, eating, playing; it comes in addition (and maybe more deeply-felt) through contact with our own physical beings.

Joy: Expanding Human Awareness is Dr. Schutz' prescription for each of us, one and all. In it he suggests, as he has to countless therapy patients and encounter groups, that we stop living in the objective, intellectual, detached, mental world that too many of us inhabit. We have minds, true; but we *are* bodies. That's not a come-down! That's a joyous realization. The book seeks to promote a re-integration of the false division between mind and body that fills most of our consciousness.

After many years of being all but ignored, the importance of body-functioning to emotional states is becoming recognized more widely and applied to growth-producing situations. A particularly fascinating discovery is the fruitfulness of certain language which, in describing emotional and behavioral states, translates almost literally into terms used to describe bodily states and functions. This translation has a profound impact on methods of dealing effectively with emotional states. A method for helping a person act out and deal with the sense of being immobilized by others, for example, is to put him in a tight circle of people and ask him to try to break out, physically. The method is based on the transformation of his *emotional* feeling of immobilization into the experience of being *physically* immobilized, to allow him the opportunity to break what he feels are unbreakable bonds. . . . But this is getting ahead of our story.

Implicit general recognition of the close connection between the emotional and the physical is evident in the verbal idioms that have developed in social interaction. Feelings and behavior are expressed in terms of all parts of the body, of body-movement, and of bodily functions. . . .

Supporting the recognition in everyday life of the close connection between bodily and emotional and mental states, there is a growing volume of theoretical work describing these connections and the way they develop and manifest themselves.

Psychosomatic medicine has made a strong case for the fact that emotional states affect the body. More recently, the opposite view has also been developed—that body-organization and physiology affect the feelings—a view called "somatopsychic." Psychological attitudes affect body-posture and functioning, and this body-formation then has a strong influence on subsequent feelings. In the theoretical work underlying a new technique, Ida Rolf[1] states it this way:

> An individual experiencing temporary fear, grief, or anger, all too often carries his body in an attitude which the world recognizes as the outward manifestation of that particular emotion. If he persists in this dramatization or consistently re-establishes it, thus forming what is ordinarily referred to as a "habit pattern," the muscular arrangement becomes set. Materially speaking some muscles shorten and thicken, others are invaded by connective tissue, still others become immobilized by consolidation of the tissue involved. Once this has happened the physical attitude is invariable; it is involuntary; it can no longer be changed basically by taking thought or even by

1. Ida Rolf, "Structural Integration," *Systematics,* Vol. 1, No. 1, June 1963. Dr. Rolf's early work was influenced by M. Feldenkrais, *Body and Mature Behavior,* New York: International Universities Press, 1949.

mental suggestion. Such setting of a physical response also establishes an emotional pattern. Since it is not possible to establish a free flow through the physical flesh, the subjective emotional tone becomes progressively more limited and tends to remain in a restricted closely defined area. Now what the individual feels is no longer an emotion, a response to an immediate situation, henceforth he lives, moves and has his being in an attitude.

Rolf describes in detail the aberrations to the physical and emotional health which may occur as a result of body imbalance:

> The man whose predominant set is fear will certainly betray it in the carriage of his head, neck, shoulders and rib cage. His defensive lack of ease will show as physical as well as psychological tension. There may be physiological imbalances of many sorts, e.g., a disturbance of the sympathetic-para-sympathetic nervous balance which must be present for the maintenance of good digestion: tensions and irregularities of the rib cage itself may become apparent as asthma, even as a disturbance of normal cardiac function. A head consistently thrust forward gives rise to an anterior displacement of the neck which will not be accessible to voluntary correction, nor to the directive: "Get your head up!" The resulting symptoms may vary from repetitive headaches to a shoulder bursitis. Various visceral functions too, can be affected through restriction of the vagus nerve.

Rolf proceeds to describe the ways in which not only emotional but physical trauma, childhood or sports accidents, etc., can also upset the body-balance. Such accidents lead to a series of bodily compensations, which may give rise to physical limitations and distortions and a feeling of weakness or instability in the body which is then transmitted to mental or emotional states.

But what is a "normal" body? What does it look like when it is functioning properly? Rolf has a very specific concept of the ideal end result of her work based on human evolution, a knowledge of the anatomy and physiology of the body, and her long experience with bodily manipulation. Normal body alignment is for the purpose of attaining these results: 1) movement is performed with minimum work, that is minimum expenditure of energy, 2) motion can be initiated in any direction with maximum ease and speed, 3) movement can start anywhere with minimum preliminary adjustment of the body, 4) structure is appropriate to the most adequate functional position of internal organs and nervous system, in other words, the organs are not crowded or unsupported, and, 5) there is minimum "wear and tear" on the parts of the body. If these criteria are attained, the body will last longer, be physically healthier, move more quickly and gracefully, have more energy and stamina, respond more quickly, and be capable of more appropriate feeling.

Alexander Lowen, a psychiatrist interested in integrating bodily and emotional states, lays great stress on the assertion that all neurotic problems are manifested in the structure and functioning of the body. This thesis implies that by proper training in what to observe, a great deal about a person may be discerned merely from looking at him. Lowen describes these connections very persuasively:[2]

> There is no neurotic problem which does not manifest itself in every aspect of the individual's function. . . . Because we express our personalities or character in every action and in every attitude it becomes possible to determine character traits from such diverse expressions as handwriting, the walk of the person, etc. . . . Most important, however, is the physical appearance at rest and in movement. No words are so clear as the language of body expression once one has learned to read it. . . .

2. A. Lowen, M.D. *Physical Dynamics of Character Structure*, New York: Grune & Stratton, 1958, pp. 87–94. Reprinted by permission. Lowen's major early influence came from Wilhelm Reich. See, for example, *Character Analysis*, New York: Orgone Institute Press, 1949.

Optimal Jones and His Wife Belle

Robert G. Amick

It is often said that only the realization that biological life is limited enables an individual to become fully involved in his own humanness and that of other persons. Technology, however, strives to create an "ideal society" through quite different means, and according to quite different criteria.

We may someday be able to create a society that is technologically perfect, with perfectly-functioning people. What new

Written especially for this anthology by Robert G. Amick.

problems of involvement may this create? This short story by Robert
Amick attempts to explore the question through a look at a society
of the future.

The small electrical current brought immediate alertness to Optimal
Jones' conscious mind. He unplugged his electrodes from the headboard,
and looked down at his still-sleeping wife. Optimal enjoyed his wife's
new face, thinking to himself that it was an improvement over the previous two. He thought, however, that the doctor had made her breasts a
little too large.

The three-dimensional television set was giving the temperature
range for the day. The announcer asked everyone to vote for the date
he wished it to rain, in order to replenish the water supply. The Weather
Control Specialists had done an outstanding job in regulating climatic
conditions, Optimal thought. Now Belle would rather lie out in the sun
than take her tanning pills. Optimal still preferred the pills because of
the more even distribution of coloring all over the body.

Optimal put on his insulated plastic body covering, and walked to
the far end of the room. He opened a cabinet and took his energy pills,
noticing that the supply was running low.

He sat down at his desk and key-punched a message to his wife:

    1) *Pick up more energy pills.*
    2) *Buy a new plastic body covering.*
    3) *Vote for rain on Monday.*
    4) *Thanks for the nice evening.*
    5) *I love you.*

Walking back to the bed, he fed the card into his wife's computer,
hearing the soft *whirr* that signified that the message was being fed into
her brain through the electrodes.

Optimal picked up his Black Box and strapped it onto his belt.
He connected his electrodes to the box and stimulated his hypothalmus.
The feeling of pleasure and well-being that washed over him assured him
that it was working.

He recalled once reading an old psychology textbook's description
of feelings of "depression". He wondered how it felt, and laughed to
himself about the primitive notions man had once had. These days, the

psychophysiobiologist, through brain implantation at birth, had virtually eliminated all such archaic, animalistic feelings as fear and anger, so that one experienced a constant euphoric state of well-being. During his adolescence, he remembered, some of the more daring boys had on occasion cross-wired their Black Boxes. They talked about how the feelings produced made them more aware of their bodies, something Optimal never quite understood. He recognized the mechanistic functions of the body for carrying one's thought processes throughout his life. But when the body wore out, the brain was transplanted to the Human Resource Computer Bank, to be kept stimulated for perpetual life. What particular value, then, to being more aware of it?

He took a last look at his wife, again appreciating the new face. He bent over her, patted her on the bottom, and kissed her goodbye.

Optimal left the apartment and walked down the hall to the air shaft. He stepped inside the bullet-shaped elevator room, fastened his safety belt, and then pressed the button for the transportation room. The sudden acceleration gave a pleasant tingle to his stomach. He remembered one time as a small boy getting sick to his stomach, because he had not yet learned how to press the Black Box to inhibit the sensation. He had regurgitated all over the inside of the elevator.

The door opened automatically. A pleasant female voice said, "Transportation room. Have a nice day." During Optimal's last body alteration, the doctor had mentioned research being done in the area of altering the vocal chords, so one could have any voice he desired. He thought this would be a great step forward. He wanted a voice with more authority—one that sounded like that of the president of his Area Commune.

The transportation room was busy. Most of the electric cars were being used. He walked over to one, but some small child had dripped his ice cream all over the seat. He chose another, drove it to the electrical magnetic track, and pushed the lever to Automatic. It would take him to the end of the area for Blue Electric Cars, where he would transfer to a Red to get to his meeting at the Area Commune Meeting Hall. Supposedly, there was to be a critical announcement at today's meeting.

As he sat back in the car, he pressed his Short-Term Memory Button until he recalled the previous evening's events. His wife had taken the Baby Boy Pill, and there was a ninety percent probability that they would have a son. They felt extremely fortunate that their application for a child had been accepted, particularly for a male. This had been an unusual year in that more couples had applied for females.

The Blue Electric Car reached its destination. Optimal stepped out of the car and found a red one available. He drove to the electrical magnetic track leading to the Area Commune Meeting Hall. It would take about a half-hour to make the trip; he set the timer on the Black Box for twenty-five minutes. He was learning his fourth language in a program sponsored by the Area Commune. He plugged one of his electrodes into the car radio and turned it on. He then stimulated the Reticular Activating System, immediately falling asleep.

As he awoke, he became conscious of the radio-teacher finishing the day's vocabulary " . . . *déjeuner,* breakfast, *déjouer,* to baffle, *délà,* beyond, *délabré,* ruined or dilapidated."

The electric car swung onto the pick-up lot. Optimal removed his electrodes. He observed that more scientists than usual seemed to be present today. Probably because of the special announcement, he thought.

He joined the group of scientists from his section. They walked to the building together, sharing bits of information. Optimal told the others that his Parenthood Application had been accepted. Everyone congratulated him. His sense of well-being was accelerated by the reaction from the others; he pressed the Inhibitory Button on the Black Box to control the over-stimulation.

Taking his seat in the Meeting Hall along with the other members of the committee, he stimulated his Optimal Level of Awareness button. The World Social Environmentalist Specialist walked to the podium and began to speak:

"Fellow scientists, I am pleased to report that this is the twenty-seventh month without a crime of violence and the seventy-second month without a murder. The only disease that has been recorded in the last thirty-two months is the 'scourge of mankind', the common cold."

This brought laughter from the audience.

"We are still overproducing food and material wealth for the entire world. There are a few problems with the Berbers from the High Atlas refusing to accept the three-dimensional television sets. The Environmental Control Specialists are trying to give them an awareness of the usefulness and pleasure of the sets through reinforcing radio programs."

As he continued to report, those present began to notice an increasingly anguished look on the face of the Physical Environmentalist Specialist, seated to the left of the speaker. He began tapping his fingers on the desk and sitting forward in his chair as the Environmentalist Control Specialist concluded his speech and returned to his seat.

There was clapping from the audience as the Physical Environmentalist Specialist took the stand. His voice cracked as he looked downward and began to speak slowly: "We have confirmed that as of 10:43 tonight, the sun's energy will reach the point of negative energy output. After that time, it will no longer be capable of supporting human life."

The Emotional Self

Words are such limiting creatures! We are insisting on the holistic approach to the study of man and his emerging self, yet our words force us to act as if we were partitioned up, separated into parts. We don't believe there is a real division between mind, body, emotion, or any other aspects of human experience. Yet, our words, our entire culture and what it does to our thinking, force us to deal with separate experiences as if they really were separate.

Here we're interested in exploring that integrated side of human selfhood that consists in, begins with, causes, and is expressed by emotions. Man's emotions are just as much a part of him as his intellect, his muscles, his digestion, and his reproduction.

Many people fail to experience themselves as significant persons because of emotional conflicts. Some, fearful of too many things, live sheltered half-lives. Others, fearful of fear itself, prance about, playing brave, bluffing, wearing a John Wayne mask that intends to fool everybody. Still others, told that anger is "bad," pretend to love and like everyone. Or they react to genuinely angerprovoking situations with a shrug and a complacent smile. They play at being "cool," for that's very big with a certain part of our society.

Though it isn't the only "troublesome" emotion, one that seems to perplex and frighten many of us is anger—the subject of both of the articles in this chapter. In the first, anthropologist and humanistic social-thinker Ashley Montagu discusses the integrated nature of man. Man is both animal and more-than-animal. Montagu is concerned that a popular idea is taking hold in the social sciences: the view that man's aggressiveness is instinctive. He criticizes the writings of Konrad Lorenz, Desmond Morris, and Robert Ardrey, which popularize and promote this view. The evidence isn't all in yet, but we invite you to read this article and compare it with the work of the men listed above.

The second article, by Barbara Kevles, attempts to establish patterns by which we can deal with our own anger and tendencies toward violence. These are not in the oversimplified how-to-do-it fashion of Dale Carnegie's books, but are relatively simple principles which we hope will invite the reader's contemplation. and application to his own life.

The Origin of Aggressiveness

Ashley Montagu

Ashley Montagu argues with the ethologists and instinct-people that man's nature not only does not contain a "germ" or "gene" that causes aggression, but man's emotional development proceeds only because of inborn needs and tendencies for co-operation.

As Montagu says, "the directiveness of the organism's activities is toward life, *not* toward death." He makes a case for intra-specific cooperation, feeling that it is part of the genetic make-up of every creature. Further, it is part of the social nature of each of us to seek out and go toward others, not to go against them.

The evidence is today overwhelming that in order to become an adequate, healthy, cooperative, loving human being it is necessary to be

Excerpt from Ashley Montagu, *The Biosocial Nature of Man*, (New York: The Grove Press, 1956), pp. 53—66. Reprinted by permission of the author.

loved. No child is born hostile or aggressive. It becomes so only when its desires to be loved and to love are frustrated, that is, when its expected satisfactions are thwarted—and the thwarting of an expected satisfaction is the definition of frustration. . . .

This is what Freud failed to perceive. What he took to be inborn hostility is, in fact, an acquired form of behavior following upon the frustration of the organism's expected satisfactions. Hostility, aggressiveness, and "bad" behavior are simply techniques for securing love, for compelling the attention of those who have refused it. While the psychophysical mechanism to develop aggressiveness as a result of the thwarting of expected satisfactions is inherited, aggressiveness as such is not inherited. The recent students of infant and child behavior are, for the most part, unanimous in agreeing that children are not born aggressive. Thus, Professor Lauretta Bender, the child psychiatrist, writes that hostility, far from being inborn, "is a symptom complex resulting from deprivations which are caused by developmental discrepancies in the total personality structure such that the constructive patterned drives for action in the child find inadequate means of satisfaction and result in amplification or disorganization of the drives into hostile or destructive aggression." "The child" she writes, "acts as though there were an inherent awareness of his needs and there is thus the expectation of having them met. A failure in this regard is a deprivation and leads to frustration and a reactive aggressive response."

Indeed, the developmental directiveness of the organism is towards maturation in terms of cooperation. Bender calls it "the inherent capacity or drive for normality." And she says, "The emphasis on the inborn or instinctive features of hostility, aggression, death wishes, and the negative emotional experiences represents a one-sided approach which has led our students of child psychology astray."

In an important study Professor A. H. Maslow has examined the viewpoint that "man's deepest impulses are bad, evil, undesirable, selfish, criminal, or otherwise reprehensible," and has found it completely wanting. Professor Maslow writes: "I find children, up to the time they are spoiled and flattened out by the culture, nicer, better, more attractive human beings than their elders, even though they are of course more 'primitive' than their elders. The 'taming and transforming' that they undergo seems to hurt rather than help. It was not for nothing that a famous psychologist once defined adults as 'deteriorated children.' "

Professor Maslow puts this viewpoint neatly: "Those human impulses," he writes, "which have seemed throughout our history to be deepest, to be most instinctive and unchangeable, to be most widely spread throughout mankind, *i.e.,* the impulse to hate, to be jealous, to be hostile, to be greedy, to be egoistic and selfish are now being discovered more and more clearly to be acquired and *not* instinctive. They are almost certainly neurotic and sick reactions to bad situations, more specifically to frustrations of our truly basic and instinct-like needs and impulses."

This, essentially, represents the viewpoint of such psychoanalysts as Karen Horney, Erich Fromm, Harry Stack Sullivan, Ives Hendrick, and many others. It is a very different viewpoint from that represented by Freud.

Is there any evidence whatever for the existence of a basic need for aggression? Is there such a thing as an aggressive drive? Has anyone ever observed "aggressive instincts," as Freud calls them, in human beings or the "love of aggression in individuals" as an expression of an "innate tendency to aggression"? I know of no one who has done so. On the other hand, the evidence indicates that the "tendency to aggression" and the "love of aggression," of which Freud and others speak, is not observable at any time in any human being who has not secondarily acquired it.

A distinguished psychiatrist, Karl Menninger, has poured scorn upon "sociologists, anthropologists, and others whose psychological groundwork is relatively deficient" for regarding aggressiveness as "the result of 'the culture' in which the individual lives. They make," he writes, "such nonsensical propositions as that all aggression is the result of frustration. Anyone who has had his toe stepped on, which is certainly not a frustration, knows how inadequate such a formula is. Furthermore it completely ignores the question of where the aggressive energy comes from which is provoked by the frustration, and this is what the instinct theory attempts to answer."

Though he denies that aggressiveness "is the result of culture" and calls nonsensical the proposition that all aggression is the result of frustration, the fact is that the relation of culture to the determinance of behavioral response could not be better illustrated than by this example of toe-stepping. For when a person living in a so-called primitive culture steps on the toes of another, he is likely to do so with bare feet upon toes that are uncornified or otherwise deformed, and is thus unlikely to hurt or frustrate the other and provoke aggressive behavior. Whereas in a culture in which one wears shoes (and bunions impede the pilgrim's progress), one is likely to hurt and frustrate the person upon whose toe one has stepped—but whether aggressiveness will be elicited or not will depend upon the manner in which the stepped-upon has learned to respond to such frustrations. If we accept the generally accepted definition of a frustration as the thwarting of an expected satisfaction, then it may perhaps be acknowledged that having one's toe stepped on may be experienced as a frustration of the expectation of pursuing the

> . . . *noiseless tenor of one's way*
> *Yet e'en these bones from insult to protect.*

We need go no further than our own culture to observe how the response to frustration is bred into one—and is therefore culturally determined. An ill-bred person may react to having his toe stepped on with aggressive behavior, a well-bred person may react with nonaggressive behavior. But this may reflect no more than a difference in the learned ability to control the expression of aggression. On the other hand, the different responses may actually represent a difference in feeling content—in the one case aggressive feeling being present and in the other not present.

Other things being equal, we can take this difference in feeling to be an expression of a nervous system which has been socialized in different ways in connection with the frequency of frustration and the training in the kind of responses permitted to them. There can be very little doubt that different culturalizing mechanisms serve to organize the nervous systems of their owners in very different ways. The evidence from different cultures of the manner in which response to frustration is trained is most impressive. Anthropologists have made the accounts of these differences so widely available that even the much-appealed-to man on the street knows that the Zuñi Indians tend to avoid every form of aggressive behavior, that the expression of aggressive behavior is institutionalized among the Kwakiutl Indians of the Northwest Pacific Coast, that the Dobuans of the Western Pacific are pathologically aggressive, and that the Arapesh of New Guinea control some forms of aggression but not others.

Where does all the aggressive energy come from that is provoked by frustration? This is usually an easy question for those to answer who have been influenced by the complex traditions which have been set out earlier in these pages. Those who pride themselves on their knowledge of evolutionary theory and those who have been influenced by that theory can always appeal to the idea that man has inherited his fund of aggressiveness from his lower animal ancestors. But *are* lower animals aggressive? Aggression is the overt expression of a feeling of hostility, and the function of the overt act is to inflict injury upon the object towards which hostility is felt. Upon occasion, probably all animals will exhibit such behavior, but the occasion has a cause. In fact, lower animals are no more innately aggressive than is man. As in man, their aggressive behavior is the response to some frustration or another. Animals do not prey upon other animals because they feel hostile towards them, even when upon occasion they may appear to "kill for killing's sake," but they do prey upon other animals in order to eat. It produces only confusion to identify predatory behavior with hostile aggressiveness as the Freudians do. In spite of Tennyson, who sang of "Nature red in tooth and claw" and the Darwinians who "proved" it, Nature is not red in tooth and claw, and it is an abysmal piece of nonsense to suggest that in a state of nature animals are in a more or less continuous state of hostility towards one another; that the lower animals are naturally aggressive; that, this being the case, man's apelike ancestors must undoubtedly have been so; and that the source of man's aggressive energies is therefore to be looked for in his lowly animal ancestry.

The Darwinian conception of competition as struggle for existence *against* other animals has assumed the form of a dogma. This dogma is more than highly questionable. Darwin himself attempted to avoid the dogma of "struggle-against" others, but often wrote as if this is what he had in mind. Darwin was quite aware of the dependence of all forms of life upon other life as a factor in survival, and that such terms as "struggle for existence" were being used by him in a metaphoric sense; but, as we all know, metaphors have a way of assuming a life of their own which often serves to take the place of the original idea—hence, the danger of all metaphors. It was a simple step to take from the idea of the "struggle-for-existence," with its origin in Malthus' "disease, famine, and war," to "fight-for-life" and "the-survival-of-the-fittest," and thus to think of "competition" as an essentially combative, violent process in which the most successful aggressor established his right to survive; hence the doctrine of "Might is Right."

It does not detract in the least from the greatness and genius of both Darwin and Freud—as well as of others—to realize that they were both so much impressed by the hostility they saw all about them that they projected this upon nature itself, but *we* do not have to make the same mistake. Man's nearest animal relatives are the gorilla and chimpanzee—they are very distant collateral relatives, indeed, and certainly not in the direct line of man's descent. They are not seen at their best behind a cage in captivity—any more than men are, but in the natural habitat to which they are accustomed they are observed to be the most peaceful of creatures. In the first place they are vegetarian and frugivorous, so that they will not harm as much as a fly. They will never attack any living creature unless they are severely provoked, as, for example, by a strange man whom they have never done the least harm who chooses to shoot at them and members of their family. When, under such conditions, the gorilla attempts to protect his family, he is described as "a ferocious beast." The real ferocious beast is not the gorilla but his unprovoked attacker—the more ferocious and the more beastly in a much more profound sense than any beast ever is, because man attacks such creatures in cold blood.

The fact is that man, unable to face it in himself, has projected his own ferocity and beastliness upon the "lower animals," who it then becomes permissible to kill because they are both beastly and ferocious. What we have made of the world of man we have projected upon the whole world of animated nature. As Pliny the Elder was the first to point out, man is the only creature in the world who makes war upon his own kind, yet we speak of "the war of nature." But nature does not make war on itself—only certain branches of mankind do. Warlike activities at the present day are unknown to many nonliterate peoples, which is one of the reasons they are called primitive and we call ourselves civilized! All the evidence indicates that war was a very late development in the history of man, not appearing until the Neolithic age, some 10,000 years ago.

What is the source, then, of the aggressive behavior of human beings if it is not from the stores of the "farfetched" energy of the "Death Instinct"? All the available evidence points to the same answer: The so-called "aggressive energy" of human beings originates in the very same source as that which supplies the energy to love. And what is that source? It is the total energy-system of the organism, an energy-system which is directed toward the achievement of living in growth and development—the birthright of every living thing. The directiveness of the organism's activities is toward life, *not* toward death.

The energy subserving the functions of love is not different from that which supplies the dynamos of aggression; the one is not a transformation of the other, it is the same energy used to achieve the same ends—the maintenance and growth of the self. Aggression *is* love—it is love frustrated. This is the relationship which Ian Suttie was among the first to point out. Suttie describes aggression as a technique or mode for compelling the attention that has been denied. Hate, Suttie suggests, is not a primal independent instinct, but a development or intensification of separation-anxiety, which in turn is evoked by a threat against love. "Hate is the maximal ultimate appeal in the child's power—the most difficult for the adult to ignore. Its purpose is not death-seeking or death-dealing, but the preservation of the self from the isolation which is death."

Since those words were published, twenty years ago, much confirmation has been brought to them by the researches of such workers as Lowrey, Levy, Goldfarb, Bender, Spitz, Bowlby, Banham, Maslow, and many others. These and other relevant researches prove that the child is dependent for its healthy development upon the love that it is given, and what is quite as important, the love that it is able to give others. From the moment of birth the infant seeks to re-establish its connection with the mother. Just as the fertilized ovum seeks to attach itself to the womb, so the newborn seeks to attach itself to the mother, and in relation to her to realize its further development—a development which is a continuation of that begun in the womb. From the first, mother and child are in a symbiotic relationship in which they confer mutually advantageous benefits upon each other. The child is as necessary for the parents' further development as is the mother for the child's development. And the tendency of the child's behavior is towards loving others. The child's need for love from others is important principally because that love is the most significant developer of its own capacity to love others.

The evidence strongly suggests that it can no longer be maintained that man is born a hostile creature or that he is born neither good nor evil, but simply indifferent, that what the human organism will become as a human being depends largely upon the kind of experience or lack of it that is offered to it. This is true to a great extent, but what does not appear to be true is that the organism is born indifferent, neither good nor evil. Indeed, the facts strongly suggest that the organism is born positively good; good in the sense that it wants to love and be loved, and it does not want to be injured or to injure. The infant is born with all its energies oriented in the direction of conferring and receiving, of exchanging, creatively enlarging benefits. The purposes of the infant are constructive—*not* destructive. He desires to live as if to live and love were one.

When the stimulations necessary to the development of his need to love and to be loved are withheld, we know that the child will generally suffer proportionately in its capacity to love. We find that when the human organism is satisfied in its expectation of love then it develops as a loving creature with a maximum tolerance for frustration and a minimum need for aggression. Aggression, it turns out, is an acquired, *not* a basic need. It is a need which is developed in the child that has not had its needs for love adequately satisfied. In such a deprived child, during its critical developmental periods, the need for love may evoke aggressive responses so frequently that the child may thus be taught aggression instead of the love in which it strives to develop its capacity. Such a child may later, as we know, use aggression whenever it wants anything. . . .

What is the nature of the behavior customarily labeled aggressive? The usual statement is that it is behavior directed toward the infliction of injury. In this meaning of the term it can safely be said that no human being has ever been born with one iota of aggression in him. In this sense it is doubtful whether any infant under six months of age ever exhibits any form of hostile aggression. The evidence indicates quite clearly that the hostile element enters, if at all, into the structure of aggression in the later stages of its development. In a study of the development of aggressive behavior in children Sears and his co-workers found no correlation between early frustration and later preschool aggression in children. They found this not surprising since, by definition, aggression is taken to be "a goal response to instigation to injure" a person, that is, a gratification arising from performing some act causing injury or pain to another. In the initial stages of the acquisition of aggression Sears and co-workers found that no more was involved "than the learning of specific acts of adaptive value that serve to remove certain kinds of interference. These acts happen to be destructive or injurious; they may be considered as instrumental rather than goal response aggression. That is, they are intended simply to aid in achieving gratification of some other drive; they are not satisfying in and of themselves. Much of the *interpersonal* aggression observed between the ages of two and four is of this character, and the true *goal response aggression* becomes noticeable, in many children, only gradually during that period."

It is absurd to regard as aggressive or destructive behavior the taking of clocks apart, the removal of the wings and legs of insects, the breaking and tearing of objects, and the other seemingly "destructive" acts in which almost every child has engaged. Observing how things work represents the expression of an extremely important stage in the development of the human being, one of whose most powerful urges is the much to be encouraged trait of curiosity. The best interests of that trait are not served by treating it as a form of aggression.

The evidence indicates that all personal aggression, whether it be of the early nonhostile variety or of the later hostile kind, is almost always the response to love frustrated and the expression of a claim upon others to provide that love. The most extreme forms of destructive aggression, as in murder, are in effect declarations of the position into which the murderer has been forced and caused, as it were, to say: If you will not love me, then I will not love you. Almost always when we witness aggressive behavior we are observing a demand for love. This is certainly the meaning of the aggressive behavior of those small infants who exhibit it—and it is equally true at all ages.

Thus understood, aggression is not best met with counter-aggression, but rather with love—for aggression is the expression of the need for love, when that love has been unfulfilled.

It is not human nature but human nurture that is the cause of human aggression. Human nature, there is every reason to believe, is good, and treated as such leads to goodness. It is necesary that we understand, in the light of the accumulated evidence, that being born into the human species means that the individual so born is capable of becoming whatever it is within the capacity of that individual to become. The social experience through which the individual passes will largely determine whether he will become a dominantly aggressive or a dominantly loving person, or someone betwixt and between. But there can be no doubt that the individual's drives are originally directed towards the achievement of love, however deformed the process of achievement may subsequently become. There can equally be little doubt that a person's drives are never oriented in a destructive direction, except in severely disturbed cases, and that such disturbances are produced principally by cultural factors.

Make Love Not War In Your Own Life

Barbara Kevles

Few feelings in the human armamentarium of emotions cause us so much trouble as anger. The earliest writings tell us that ancient men wrestled with this problem as well.

Anger is not bad. It can and often does lead to bad behaviors. But it can also lead to good behaviors, as those who enjoy making up after a quarrel will testify. Here, Barbara Kevles presents her ideas about the place of anger and violence in our lives.

When America watched the violence televised from the Democratic Convention, most of the affluent made no connection between Chicago and their own lives. How absurd! Acts of violence happen not only beyond the hedges, the picket fences, the front doors of the middle class, but smack in their own homes. In perfectly proper families, parents beat children to a pulp; teen-agers wreck the family car on purpose; sons and daughters are evicted from their homes.

"Proper" families breed violence by substituting status symbols for love. Hugs, approval, encouragement are earned by children for doing things: keeping a stylish appearance at the family affair, scoring high grades—and are earned by parents for giving things: a Corvair for Christmas, a fun fur for the college campus. When *things* are substituted for expressing feelings, families bottle up what they want to say. Talk bottled long enough explodes into violence.

Violence: Last Resort at Communication

Violence is expressed in many ways. *The Oxford Dictionary* defines it: "Physical force to inflict injury or damage upon persons or property." How can a nice girl from a nice home destroy her mother's kitchen? How can a well brought-up boy knife a brother?

Nice girls and boys are better trained at keeping up appearances than at expressing their feelings. To most of us the language of pain is as foreign as Ubangi. Bankrupt of words to defend feelings, those hurt seem to have only one alternative to get their point across—violence. Violence is a message that often is not understood.

Some authorities extend the definition of violence beyond the physical to include the psychological impact: A white boy brings home a Negro girl and is disowned.

A girl caught sleeping with a married man is commanded by her parents to shoot her dog and, instead, shoots herself.

There are infinite ways of inflicting pain without touching. This covert violence avoids the issue. We don't have to confront the people we depend upon with our grievances. This is underground guerrilla warfare in the recreation room.

Rickie can't wait for next fall because then she moves out of the posh Manhattan apartment shared with mother (a divorcée) and into the dormitory at New York University. She and her mother battle daily. After one particularly brutal argument, mother explodes emotionally and sends Rickie to an aunt in Long Island for the summer. Long Island is Squaresville. Rickie is boxed in, frustrated, abandoned. One afternoon, she stood before the bathroom mirror and gulped down a quinine pill, than another, than several. But when the pain became excruciating, she called the doctor. Why had she tried suicide?

Rickie tried to get through to her mother, but mother discouraged the criticism with "Because . . ." or "I'm your mother, that's why . . ." or "As long as you live under my roof . . ." We are not taught how to criticize our family or, for that matter, ourselves. The rage that had bottled up for years inside Rickie finally turned on her.

Rickie receives help now from a psychiatrist twice a week. Through these sessions she is coming to understand how much she needs her mother and, what she didn't know, *how much her mother needs her.*

The first time Rickie's mother visited her in the hospital when she was recovering from her suicide attempt, she confessed failure as a parent. They both cried. She asked her mother to trust her even when she is making mistakes, on the faith she'll outgrow her hangups. Rickie says, "Our meeting was like a scene from a soap opera, but we've never been the same since."

Is talking about a problem a solution or a stopgap? Are we born with innate violence? Dr. Frederick Wertham, an authority on human violence, says, "No. Violence is learned behavior. It is not an instinct like sex or hunger. Animals do not kill for hate, spite, revenge, sadism or greed. Most important of all, they never systematically kill large numbers of the same species. So when we speak of massacres, extermination camps, mass bombings . . . we should not refer to the 'bestial' in man. It isn't the beast, it is man itself. . . ."

Most animals have an inborn mechanism that prevents such beasts of prey as wolves or lions from killing members of their pack. Man has such an instinctive drive, too. Unfortunately, this instinct against killing his kind has been smothered by his deluxe weapon arsenal. Man's power to kill man has grown beyond his control.

But, we are not *inherently* violent. Wertham states that when a person prepares to threaten or carry out a violent act, a part of his lower brain is stimulated. But the violent urge, Wertham stresses, "can be inhibited by higher centers in the brain, the cerebral cortex."

How can we control violence in America when television, magazines, newspapers continually tell us violence is masculine?

And what is a man? Everywhere a boy looks, in most of the mass media, to be a man is to be cool, show no emotions, use physical violence. If a boy learns he-men solve problems with fists, why shouldn't he? Yet when John Glenn returned after the first man-flight in space, he cried when he saw his wife. One may catch the John Glenns of our society in a two-minute news clip, at best, while the groovy nighttime serials feature the hand-to-holster heroes in saturation. Those are society's models—men who, when they kill, never grimace or cry. So, boys try to be men with their fists.

Anthony Storr, one of Britain's most articulate psychiatrists and a man steeped in the studies of ethology—animal instinct under natural conditions—defines aggression as "a drive as innate, as natural and as powerful as sex." Freud branded the aggressive drive as what led man toward destruction and death. Today Storr and others disagree with

Freud. They emphasize aggression is essential for survival and mastery of the environment. Storr writes in his book, *Human Aggression,* "In adult life, the aggressive drive which in childhood enables the individual to break free of parental domination serves to preserve and define identity." On constructive control of aggression's destructive impulses, Storr guardedly warns, "There is no clear dividing line between those forms of aggression which we all deplore and those which we must not disown if we are to survive."

It's startling to speak of love in the same breath with aggression, but the facts prove aggression is essential to lovemaking. The "passive woman in sex" myth is very unsatisfactory if followed. The best possible outlet for the ever-increasing stockpile of aggression is love. Konrad Lorenz, father of modern ethology, thinks only animals capable of intense aggression are capable of intense personal ties and love since the aggressive instinct can be the energy for violence, or, redirected, the same energy can be transformed into acts of love.

In the course of writing this article, I participated involuntarily in a revealing act of violence. A friend, Barbara Connell, her husband and I were watching President Johnson announce his latest bid for peace in Vietnam and his decline to run again for the President. I persisted in making asides.

When it was all over, Barbara, who is a Democrat's Democrat, verbally attacked me, "You weren't listening from the top. You're the kind of person who approaches a situation with preconceived notions. You're one of millions of negative people who see nothing good about this country."

Rather than give vent to my anger at her, I stalked out of the house and spent the next half hour walking. When I returned, I refused to talk about Johnson, the war or my cousins in Vietnam. Barbara tried to force me to say what was bothering me. I wouldn't. I had to be polite. Barbara grabbed my shoulders and shook me, shouting, "Do you want to be my friend, do you? Then tell me what you feel."

Then, though fearful of losing the friendship, I came out and accused Barbara of maligning me. She apologized and I apologized, too, for being supersensitive. Once we said what we *really felt,* once we aired hostilities, the tension eased. After arguing, we both felt a deeper communication, a sense of ultra-frequency contact—a real high.

From this, an epiphany: It's not enough to cool it, to not act violently. The way to love other people is to express what we feel—anger and love—without aiming to hurt feelings. Open but reverent communication is how to make love in our lives.

How to Deal with Violence in Your Own Life

1. Stop playing the role of victim in your family. Step out of the role of child-student and take the role of guru-adult. Start a rap going with your parents over mutual pain points. If they've criticized your appearance, for example, compliment them on their concern for your well-being, then criticize them by opening with "I know you didn't mean to, but . . ." "You might have said . . ." "Did you consider my feelings when you . . . ?" As long as you both show respect for each other, very difficult areas can be discussed rationally.

2. When someone hurts you, express what you feel immediately. Say: "I was embarrassed by"

"You put me down when"

"I was jealous of"

"I was hurt by"

"I tried to . . . but you wouldn't listen."

3. When you criticize someone else, be prepared to take some artillery fire in return. It is frightening, sometimes terrifying, to have it out because when you attack, you must also expose your vulnerabilities. Don't hold back. As poet Kahlil Gibran said: "Pain breaks the shell of understanding."

4. When you become so enraged you cannot speak in normal conversational terms, YELL!

5. If you are always put down at home, find an outlet elsewhere that will give you an intake of self-esteem. Educated people are desperately needed to help the ghetto poor. Inquire into projects where you could make a real contribution and boost *your* ego.

6. If you hear the same criticisms time and again, don't tune out on your critic. Confront and try to discover the real reasons. You may learn you have a fault, or that it is a sign of insecurity in the other person projected on you.

7. Read Dr. Fredrick Wertham's book, *A Sign for Cain: An Exploration of Human Violence; Joy* by William C. Schutz, and *Human Aggression* by Anthony Storr.

8. Whoever you are, when you have the urge to cry, *cry!*

9. When you sense you are the victim of some form of covert violence, don't ignore the fact. It may pain you to know someone dislikes you, but try to find out why.

10. When you want to express anger, begin with "I feel," not "You are." Direct accusations put people on the defensive at a time when you want them to be most open.

11. Stop pretending movie and television violence has no relationship to you. Evaluate fast-draw and fist-to-chin solutions: Do they really work as problem-*solving* devices?

12. If violence has already erupted between you and someone else, remember it is a form of communication. Try to tune in to the message: *Who* is trying to tell you *what?* That's a beginning.

The Social Self

Man is that complex creature who is both an individual unit and a functional and integral part of the social units to which he belongs. We are born into groups and we never lose our social feeling. We experience our selfhood most fully when we can effectively integrate our individual existences into our social lives. Adler calls this "social interest," and tells us that this paradoxical realization is the healthiest way of living.

Cooperation and competition are processes that all of us experience. Conflict is a further extension of competition. We are under the necessity of finding ways of integrating all of these processes realistically and effectively into our growing sense of self.

Alexander Eulenspiegel speaks of the role of individuation in our lives in his article, "The Individual," taken from the *Los Angeles Free Press.* Man is in a crisis today, partly because neither his individuality nor his social feeling is well developed.

Hermann Hesse, the sensitive and thought-provoking German novelist, has captured the imaginations of many college students in the past few years, as he did older people in the 1930's and '40's. In the excerpt from *Demian,* the young hero, Emil Sinclair, discovers the depth of his involvement in society, when he discovers the power another person can have over his thoughts and actions.

The Individual: A Matter of Life and Death

Alexander Eulenspiegel

Is the individual only an isolated unit? Does a man have to lose his identity, his sense of self, to belong to the group? Is there only this choice of "either-or"?

Eulenspiegel is a thoughtful and sensitive writer. In this article he tries to give us the necessary perspective to appreciate both our individual identity *and* our social roles.

There is a widespread notion that Western civilization holds each individual human life precious, while Orientals and other savages around the globe view life as cheap. Buddhism and Hinduism teach that the individual is nothing; therefore starvation and disease run wild in India, and the Japanese are a cruel, violent, suicidal, homicidal people. On the other hand, according to this notion, the Hebrew-Greek-Christian ethical tradition has taught Western man that the individual is precious and irreplaceable, and our medicine, legal system, agriculture and technology all work to keep each individual in Western society alive and healthy.

The truth is, the Western attitude toward death is schizophrenic in the extreme. The Eastern attitude, given the actual human condition, is more realistic and perhaps healthier.

Today I heard about the killing of a 25-year-old photographer in New York City. He was taking pictures of a girl model in Mod clothing against a contrasting slum background on the Lower East Side. A group of kids came along. One kid felled the photographer with a window

Alexander Eulenspiegel, "The Individual," first printed in *Los Angeles Free Press*, May 23, 1969, p. 13. Reprinted with the kind permission of the publisher.

sash; then some others jumped on him and stabbed him to death. When I heard this, I was stunned, saddened, and chilled. I wanted to know everything about the incident, every detail, anything that could point toward an explanation. Did they want to steal his camera? Had he provoked them? Were they speed freaks? Was it class resentment, pure and simple?

I started thinking about what a damned shame it is to be 25 years old, talented, skilled, doing interesting work and suddenly be dead after a one-minute street fight. I was really identifying with that young photographer; I was really down. But, like Boethius, I am consoled by philosophy, and I remembered what I'd read in *The Book,* in other works by Watts, in Huxley, in Suzuki, in others who retail Oriental philosophy to all of us who can't speak or read Sanskrit, Chinese, or Japanese. Death is not an absolute, tragic calamity to be fended off at all costs. Life is a game with no point outside itself, and death is merely the withdrawal of a player from the game, after which there is nothing, neither regret nor triumph. The notion that we are individuals and that our egos are infinitely precious is an illusion. We are not individuals, and our desire to survive as individuals is as silly as it would be if a leaf insisted on clinging permanently to a tree.

Thoughts like these enable me to take the young man's death in stride, to go on about my business without getting bogged down in sorrow and horror. They also enable me to dismiss the intimations of my own mortality implicit in the incident.

But—isn't such an attitude precisely what is wrong with Oriental philosophy? Is it not a glory of our Western civilization that we recoil in horror before the death of a single person? But we don't always recoil in horror; sometimes we barely notice. It depends on who the person is. Several years ago I attended a press luncheon given by Dick Gregory's publishers to launch his autobiography, *Nigger.* Just around that time a bunch of white missionary hostages had been massacred by Congolese rebels, and Gregory remarked that he was not especially moved by their deaths. A lady reporter expressed disapproval and incredulity. Gregory replied that there were thousands of black Africans being killed every day in those same Congo troubles, and the press treated them as mere numbers. But when the white missionaries were killed, shock and outrage thundered around the world. So Dick Gregory just didn't care.

If a black man is stabbed to death in a ghetto, the press treats it as just another cuttin' in darktown. Similarly, it is hardly possible to get one-half of one percent of the people in this country to protest the deaths of hundreds of thousands of Vietnamese civilians which are the direct result of American action in that country. What happens to our respect for individual life in these cases?

This Hebrew-Greek-Christian civilization which puts such a high value on human life has quite a record. It includes the Biblical Moses who, when the armies of Israel brought Midianite prisoners to him, "was wroth," and said, "Have ye saved all the women alive? . . . Now therefore, kill every male among the little ones, and kill every woman that hath known man by lying with him." It includes Athens, which manages to be described as the world's first democracy because everyone forgets that eighty percent of the population were non-citizens or slaves. It includes the Christianity of the Middle Ages which executed nine million people for witchcraft and millions more for heresy and made a regular practice of wiping out whole communities of Jews.

With the transition from the Middle Ages to the Renaissance, we he-men of Europe carried our civilization with its high respect for human life to various barbarous peoples overseas. The Spaniards taught it to the Aztecs by killing 15 million Indians during the first years of their conquest of the New World. Our United States of America, second to none in proclaiming the sanctity of individual lives, exterminated Indians and enslaved Africans in order to take over the North American continent. Colonization and extermination marched on through the eighteenth and nineteenth centuries; the entire population of Tasmania wiped out; the Belgians in the Congo behaved like the Nazis in Poland; the British fought a war to force the importation of opium into China.

But it is in the twentieth century that Western civilization really hit its stride. Our solicitude for lives and the technological progress bred by this concern has never been more apparent or more gloriously successful. We have proven our superiority to the Orient in medicine, agriculture and industry. Whereas in the East people are nothing but anonymous masses, we take care of human beings. We have also perpetrated the two most gigantic, bloodiest wars in human history; in the second one we killed 30 million people. We bombed cities out of existence, and by the end of the war we were able to do this with a single bomb (which we used on those Orientals who set no value on human life). We have now arrived at a pinnacle on which we are at work on four distinct ways of wiping out the human race: nuclear warfare, chemical-biological warfare, overpopulation and pollution of the atmosphere of the entire planet.

With his eyes on the heavenly ideal of the sanctity of human life, Western man fails to see that he is up to his waist in blood.

What this contradiction suggests to me is that our culture does not value life at all. Instead, we fear death. Death, we have been taught, is the ultimate catastrophe, from which there is no appeal. Death is the worst tragedy of all, however, only for me and for people like me (since if death can get people like me, it can get *me*). The whole world is divided into Us and Them, and the death of one of Them is of no importance at all.

This is manifested in the way the press treats some deaths as disasters of the first magnitude, while others are barely mentioned. It is even more vividly apparent in the movies. When certain characters die, the event is milked for all the emotion it can evoke; the horror of the sadness is drawn out, played upon, multiplied. Other characters—Indians, outlaws, natives, enemy soldiers—die in the blink of an eye, and a blink is about the extent of our reaction to these deaths.

Both attitudes are out of proportion. In contrast, the Oriental way looks like a middle way. No one who has seen photographs of Vietnamese women weeping over their dead children has to be told that the Oriental view of life and death is far from being a callous, inhuman attitude. On the other hand, Orientals do not seem to look on death as some sort of unnatural outrage that should be abolished by the next medical discovery.

Norman O. Brown thinks Freud was right when he said that man has an innate desire to die. Like any other instinct, Brown points out in *Life Against Death,* when this desire is repressed it makes trouble. Much of Hindu and Buddhist philosophy, it seems to me, is aimed at inculcating a serene accepting of one's own death, and a predictable concomitant of that will be a rather calm feeling about the deaths of others. Oriental civilizations never developed the marvelous life-saving technology ours has, but neither have they killed people on the same scale or menaced all human life the way Western technology has done. In the West we repress the death instinct. We build a civilization which works overtime to stave off death for a relative handful of people, and we glorify what we do for this handful by saying that we, unlike other cultures, have a unique concern for the preciousness of individual human life. And when the economy and technology we have built to protect us actually causes the deaths of millions more people, we simply look the other way.

We are always either staring at death in fascinated horror or looking the other way. It seems a bit much to expect people to actually desire death (which, I suppose, would be the expression of an unrepressed death instinct). But we might, more of us, try to come to terms with the fact, as I think Oriental philosophers have, that life without death is the sound of one hand clapping.

Sinclair Discovers Life

Hermann Hesse

Life often sneaks up on us, especially some of the more mysterious or hidden aspects of life. Emil Sinclair, a young boy, discovers how deep and powerful life's forces are. He has stolen some apples from an orchard, and seemingly has gotten away with it. But an older boy, Franz Kromer, saw him and is now tormenting him with threats that he will inform on the younger boy if he doesn't pay him money. Sinclair pays what he can. The pattern is set. Daily, there are more and bigger demands for blackmail payments.

But Sinclair has met another older boy, Max Demian. Demian has a strange power, a confidence and insight, that draws Sinclair to him. In the excerpt from Hermann Hesse's novel *Demian*, we see young Sinclair as he suddenly confronts another of the realities of life, the sexual side.

I couldn't even get upstairs. My life was wrecked. I thought of running away and never coming back, or of drowning myself. However, I couldn't picture any of this very clearly. In the dark, I sat down on the bottom step of our staircase, huddled up within myself, abandoning myself to misery. That's where Lina found me weeping as she came down-'stairs with the basket to fetch wood.

I begged her not to say a word, then I went upstairs. To the right of the glass door hung my father's hat and my mother's parasol; they gave me a feeling of home and comfort, and my heart greeted them thankfully, as the Prodigal Son might greet the sight and smell of old familiar rooms. But all of it was lost to me now, all of it belonged to the clear, well-lighted world of my father and mother and I, guilty and deeply engulfed in an alien world, was entangled in adventures and sin, threatened by an enemy,—by dangers, fear, and shame. The hat and parasol, the old sandstone floor I was so fond of, the broad picture above the hall cupboard, the voice of my elder sister coming to me from the living room were all more moving, more precious, more delicious than ever before, but they had ceased to be a refuge and something I could rely on; they had become an unmistakable reproach. None of this was mine any more, I could no longer take part in its quiet cheerfulness. My feet had become muddied, I could not even wipe them clean on the mat; everywhere I went I was followed by a darkness of which this world of home knew nothing. How many secrets I had had, how often I had been afraid—but all of it had been child's play compared with what I brought home with me today. I was haunted by misfortune, it was reaching out toward me so that not even my mother could protect me, since she was not even allowed to know. Whether my crime was stealing or lying—(hadn't I sworn a false oath by God and everything that was sacred?)—was immaterial. My sin was not specifically this or that but consisted of having shaken hands with the devil. Why had I gone along? Why had I obeyed Kromer—better even than I had ever obeyed my father? Why had I invented the story, building myself up with a crime as though it were a heroic act? The devil held me in his clutches, the enemy was behind me.

For the time being I was not so much afraid of what would happen tomorrow as of the horrible certainty that my way, from now on, would lead farther and farther downhill into darkness. I felt acutely that new offenses were bound to grow out of this one offense, that my presence among my sisters, greeting and kissing my parents, were a lie, that I was living a lie concealed deep inside myself.

For a moment, hope and confidence flickered up inside me as I gazed at my father's hat. I would tell him everything, would accept his verdict and his punishment, and would make him into my confessor and savior. It would only be a penance, the kind I had often done, a bitterly difficult hour, a ruefully difficult request for forgiveness.

How sweet and tempting that sounded! But it was no use. I knew I wouldn't do it. I knew I now had a secret, a sin which I would have to expiate alone. Perhaps I stood at the parting of the ways, perhaps I would now belong among the wicked forever, share their secrets, depend on them, obey them, have to become one of their kind. I had acted the man and hero, now I had to bear the consequences.

Presumably, my parents also were distressed by the state I was in. A strange spirit had taken hold of me, I no longer fitted into our community, once so intimate; yet often a wild longing came over me to return to it as to a lost paradise. My mother in particular treated me more like an invalid than a scoundrel, but my true status within the family I was better able to judge from my sisters' attitude. Theirs was one of extreme indulgence, which made it plain that I was considered a kind of madman, more to be pitied for his condition than blamed, but possessed by the devil nonetheless. They prayed for me with unusual fervor and I was infinitely miserable when I realized the futility of these prayers. Often I felt a burning need for relief, for genuine confession, and yet sensed in advance that I would be unable to tell my mother or father, and explain everything sympathetically, that they would, yes, even feel sorry for me, but that they would not understand, that the whole thing would be regarded as a momentary aberration, whereas in truth it was my fate.

I realize that some people will not believe that a child of little more than ten years is capable of having such feelings. My story is not intended for them. I am telling it to those who have a better knowledge of man. The adult who has learned to translate a part of his feelings into thoughts notices the absence of these thoughts in a child, and therefore comes to believe that the child lacks these experiences, too. Yet rarely in my life have I felt and suffered as deeply as at that time.

One day it rained. Kromer had ordered me to meet him at the Burgplatz, and there I stood and waited, shuffling among the wet chestnut leaves that were still falling from the black wet trees. I had no money with me but I had managed to put aside two pieces of cake and had brought them along so as to be able to give Kromer something at least. By now, I was used to standing in some corner and waiting for him, often a very long time, and I accepted in the same way one learns to put up with the inevitable.

Kromer showed up finally. He didn't stay long. He poked me in the ribs a few times, laughed, took the cake, even offered me a damp cigarette (which, however, I did not accept), and was friendlier than usual.

"Yes," he said nonchalantly before going away, "before I forget it, you might bring your sister along the next time, the older one, what's her name."

I failed to get his point and made no reply. I only looked at him, surprised.

"Don't you understand? You're to bring your sister."

"No, Kromer, that's impossible. I wouldn't be allowed to and she wouldn't come in any case."

I was prepared for this new ruse or pretext of his. He did this often: demanded something impossible, frightened and humiliated me, then gradually offered some bargain as a way out, and I had to buy myself off with some money or a gift.

This time, however, it was altogether different. My refusal did not seem to make him angry at all.

"Well, anyway," he said in a matter-of-fact tone, "think it over. I'd like to meet your sister. We'll find a way one of these days. You could simply take her along on a walk and then I could join you. I'll give you a whistle tomorrow, then we can talk about it some more."

After he had left, something of the nature of his request suddenly dawned on me. I was still quite ignorant in these matters but I knew from hearsay that boys and girls when they grew older were able to do certain mysterious, repulsive, forbidden things together. And now I was supposed to—it suddenly flashed on me how monstrous his request was! I knew at once that I would never do it. But what would happen then? What revenge would Kromer take on me? I didn't dare think of it. This was the beginning of a new torture for me.

Inconsolable, I walked across the desolate square, hands in my pockets. Further and greater agonies awaited me!

Suddenly a vigorous cheerful voice called me. I was startled and began to flee. Someone ran after me, a hand grasped me gently from behind. It was Max Demian.

"Oh, it's you," I said mistrustfully. "You gave me a terrible shock."

He looked down at me and never had his look been more adult, superior, the look of someone who could see through me. We had not spoken to each other for a long time.

"I feel sorry for you," he said in his polite yet decisive manner. "Listen, you can't let yourself be frightened like that."

"Well, one can't always help it."

"So it seems. But look: if you practically go to pieces in front of someone who hasn't done you any harm, then that someone begins to think. He's surprised, he becomes inquisitive, he thinks you're remarkably high-strung and reaches the conclusion that people are always like that when they're deathly afraid. Cowards are constantly afraid, but you're not a coward, are you? Certainly, you're no hero either. And that should never be, you should never be afraid of men. You aren't afraid of me? Or are you?"

"Oh, no, not at all."

"Exactly. But there are people you are frightened of?"

"I don't know. . . . Why don't you let me be?"

He kept pace with me—I had quickened my steps with thoughts of escaping—and I felt him glancing at me from the side.

"Let's assume," he began again, "that I don't mean to do you any harm. At any rate, you've no need to be afraid of me. . . . There must be things and people that you're afraid of. If you are afraid of someone, the most likely reason is that this someone has something on you. For example, you've done something wrong and the other person knows it— he has a hold on you. You get it? Very clear isn't it?"

The Working and Creative Self

Often we think of our living existences as apart from our loves, our marriage, our work, our fun, our creative activities. Pity. We make the point that, in our society at least, we can both discover and express our significant selfhood in these very areas. It isn't a question of "which came first, the self or the expression?" This makes it more of a battle than we think discovering and expressing selfhood has to be.

Many people today are questioning the nature and place of work in our culture. But few will deny that we have all been raised to believe that a man's worth is integrally tied to his work ability and productivity.

The Puritan Ethic, or Work-Sin Ethic, makes most of us work in a compulsive way, either out of duty or obligation or else out of fear that idleness is a mark of "sinfulness" or unworthiness. Many people enjoy their labors and find fulfillment and self-expression in their work experiences. Many people are extremely creative in their laboring, adding to the richness and fullness of their own lives and those of their society.

We have selected two portions of literature for you that will illustrate some of the controversial aspects of work and of creativity. In Don Fabun's article, he illustrates some of the personal and social characteristics of the creative person. Fabun, Director of Publications for Kaiser Aluminum and Chemical Corporation, writes in a crisp and fascinating style and is, in our thinking, one of the best examples of his own subject.

In the second selection, theologian Harvey Cox tells us what work has become in the Secular City.

The Creative Person:
He Walks Alone Upon the Midnight

Don Fabun

What characterizes the creative person? Is he necessarily artistic? Does he look or talk or act in a particular way? Does he fit any of our contemporary stereotypes?

Don Fabun feels that several key traits are found in all creative individuals, whether they are artists, machinists, carpenters, teachers, or executives.

In this excerpt from his publication *You and Creativity,* we find that the creative traits are well within the range of possibility for any of us, but that for most of us they have been hidden or limited by our upbringing, our experiences, and our own self-imposed doubts.

Who is this stranger that walks in upon us and upsets our lives? From whence comes the man who "marches to a different drummer," to whom the cherished wisdom of the ages is but chaff upon the wind? Why is he so different? Or is he really so different after all? Is he not perhaps only like ourselves, except that he has kept something we have lost along the way? Who, and what, is the "creative person"?

To begin with, it is not certain there is such a creature; we have a semantic difficulty here. "Ordinary" persons may be highly creative under certain circumstances—as witness the performance of people in concentration or prisoner-of-war camps. On the other hand, quite gifted persons may not do anything essentially creative—i.e., may not form original patterns in a whole lifetime, but will cling to the safe and accepted. History is full of them.

Yet, somehow, the creative person does seem to be different from most other people.

For one thing, of course, he exhibits creativity at a fairly high rate. He is the one society instinctively turns to when it needs "new" ideas. It doesn't matter, of course, whether society asks or not; the creative person will turn them out anyway. If one studies the life stories of highly creative people, it appears obvious that there are certain similarities in their background and in their personalities. But, being creative, they are also quite different from each other. "The full and complete picturing of the creative person will require many images," says Donald W. MacKinnon in "What Makes a Person Creative?" *(Saturday Review,* February 10, 1962).

Here is an outline of one image that emerges—oversimplified, to be sure, more a caricature than a portrait:

1. Inherited Sensitivity—

a propensity for a greater sensitivity to certain types of experience—mathematical, artistic, musical, mechanical, literary. This appears to be well established by studies of families which exhibit high creativity in certain fields over several generations.

"Possibly," Seidel says, "the artist's apparently odd way of looking at things derives more from the inherited and developed sensitivity which makes him more readily attuned to the subtleties of various sensations and impressions, than from an asymmetrical viewpoint different from the ordinary man in the street . . . The peculiar way the creative person may look at things derives from a physically based sensitivity toward sensations of a certain type."

2. Early Training—

the creative person, more likely than not, had his childhood in a home atmosphere that encouraged, rather than discouraged, inquisitiveness (although too rigid a home environment might drive him to seek new and original answers on his own). Creativity is as much a matter of attitude as anything, and most human attitudes may be imprinted before the age of seven.

3. Liberal Education—

the creative person is more likely to express his creativity if he is exposed to teachers and curricula that place a premium upon questions rather than answers, and which reward curiosity rather than learning by rote and conformity.

4. Asymmetrical Ways of Thought—

the creative person finds an original kind of order in disorder; it is as if he stared at the reflection of nature in a distorted mirror, where "ordinary" people are able only to see the image in a plain mirror. Most highly intelligent people (as measured by tests) have symmetrical ways of thought, and for them, everything balances out in some logical way.

5. Personal Courage—

the creative person is not afraid of failure, or of being laughed at. He can afford this risk because what is important—to him—is not what others think of him, but what he thinks of himself.

6. Sustained Curiosity—

the creative person never stops asking questions, even of his most cherished ideas. "Those who have an excessive faith in their ideas," said Claude Bernard, "are not well fitted to make discoveries." A capacity for childlike wonder, carried into adult life, typifies the creative person.

7. Not Time-Bound—

morning, noon and night are all the same to the creative person; he does not work by the clock. Problems may take years to solve, discovery may take decades. With his personal "window of infinity," time has a personal, not a social meaning. Truly creative persons seldom respond well to "deadlines" arbitrarily set by someone else.

8. Dedication—

an unswerving desire to do something, whatever it may be and whatever the obstacles to doing it. The problem will not be left unsolved; the feeling will not remain unexpressed.

9. Willingness To Work—

it is quite possible that no one in our society works harder than the artist; the same may be said for the creative scientist, inventor, composer or mathematician. This may not express itself in the number of hours put in on the job, or in obvious physical labor, but in the fact that even in sleep or reverie the creative person is constantly working for a solution. The willingness to spend years simply accumulating data about which a creative question may be asked (Darwin is a good example; so is Edison) is characteristic of the creative person.

It might also be said that the creative person is usually "intelligent" but that the intelligent person is not necessarily creative. For one thing, the tests for determining each measure quite different abilities and so are hard to compare. Intelligence tests mostly ask for the "right" answers; already predetermined. Tests for creativity most frequently ask for original answers and the degree by which they depart from the expected is a measure of their creativity.

Finally, and this seems to be largely true, the creative person is more interested in ideas and things than he is in personal relationships. When B. S. Bloom at the University of Chicago set up two groups—all of whom were chemists or mathematicians—those who were considered creative by their colleagues and those who were not, he could, out of 27 tests given each, find only two differences of any importance. One was that the creative group was made up of extremely hardworking people; and the second was that they tended to be more asocial than social. Other tests have shown that one characteristic of the creative person is that he will almost always, given the prior information, choose an answer that is the opposite to the majority.

So far we have talked about the creative person as if he existed in some sort of vacuum; a creature strange by "normal" standards who stands apart from the herd, thinking his own thoughts and going his own way. But you cannot separate an organism from its environment and expect to understand very much about it. Creativity, as we have said, is an original transaction between an organism and its environment, and for most human beings that environment is the culture in which they find themselves embedded, like an insect in amber.

In some cultures, the creative act may be rewarded by burning at the stake, being hanged or beheaded, or so thoroughly ostracized by the community as to delay the consideration and the acceptance of the creative product by decades or centuries. It may, as some of us remember, lead to crucifixion.

Certainly, there appear to be societies and cultures in which creativity is encouraged or suppressed. One thinks immediately of the difference between the Renaissance and the "Dark Ages," although these are retrospective judgments and it may be that each was, in its own way, equally creative, but that in our times we value the created products of one more than another.

In any event, to return to our original point, "Culture is the matrix and the context for creativity; indeed, it is the context for all creative behavior," says Morton I. Teicher in *Culture and Creativity.* "Culture, elaborated and developed, makes creativity possible, and in turn, is enriched by creativity. The relationship between culture and creativity is a reciprocal relation of interdependence."

"You can never localize creativity as a subjective phenomenon," says Rollo May, "You can never study it in terms simply of what goes on in a person . . . For what is occurring is always a process, a doing; specifically, a process interrelating the person and his world."

As A. L. Kroeber, in *Configurations of Cultural Growth,* has pointed out, "The nature and number of creative productions shows great variations between cultures and within the same culture at different times."

Is it possible to outline what the characteristics of a culture must be if it is to exhibit a high degree of creativity among the people who live in it at a certain time? We have tried to sketch the creative person; why not the creative society? Let's try. Characteristics of a creative society (or institution within a society, such as business corporations, the church, the government, education, etc.) may be:

(1) Generation of sufficient material wealth to provide time and opportunity for the creative process. Persons involved solely in subsistence are unlikely to exhibit much creativity; their daily lives are focused by the conscious on sheer survival.

(2) A communication system that allows a variety of inputs and free exchange of outputs between members. Societies and institutions that keep things "secret" stifle creativity because the amount of accessible information on which original patterns may be produced has been restricted.

It seemed to me that much boiled down to the relative absence of fear (in creative persons) . . . They seemed to be less afraid of what other people would say or demand or laugh at . . . Perhaps more important, however, was their lack of fear of their own insides, of their own impulses, emotions, thoughts.

—Abraham Maslow
"Creativity in Self-Actualizing People"

To be creative, in short, is to be unpredictable; it is to be decidedly suspect in the world of affairs. The creative aspect of life is rightly viewed as action. Never simply contemplative, the creative act at its highest brings about notable differences in things, thoughts, works of art and social structures. What is to be changed fights back; perhaps with success.

—George D. Stoddard
"Creativity in Education"

What are the conditions of the creative attitude, of seeing and responding, of being aware and being sensitive to what one is aware of? First of all, it requires the capacity to be puzzled. Children still have the capacity to be puzzled . . . But once they are through the process of education, most people lose the capacity of wondering, of being surprised. They feel they ought to know everything, and hence that it is a sign of ignorance to be surprised or puzzled by anything.

—Erich Fromm

Henry Eyring commented, "A keen observer once said of Einstein that part of his genius was his inability to understand the obvious" (in "Scientific Creativity").

Sidney Parnes once said, "Our discipline is the unknown; the mind has a window toward infinity."

With me, a picture is a sum of destructions. I make the picture, and proceed to destroy it. But in the end nothing is lost; the red I have removed from one part shows up in another.

—Pablo Picasso
"Conversations avec-Picasso"

Eugene Speicher likened painting to playing with electricity. "Touch one part of the canvas," he said, "and something immediately happens to some other part."

(3) A reward system in which the creative act may be socially and economically rewarded. Much of the creative talent of the world has been wasted because of societies that kept artists in poverty, inventors in ill-equipped laboratories, scientists on bare subsistence.

(4) A climate of acceptability rather than punishment for creative acts; if punishment is too severe, or too certain, creativity may not be thwarted, but the availability of the created product may be long delayed.

(5) Opportunities for privacy; research in non-interruptive surroundings, time for individual meditation, escape from disruption by family, friends, or colleagues is essential to the creative process. Many societies do not provide sanctuaries of any kind.

(6) Ability to form disciple or peer groups, such as art colonies, professional associations, conventions under conditions which favor free association of people with similar interests. These afford intensive environments where individuals may inspire each other.

(7) An educational system that rewards and encourages free inquiry, rather than acting solely as a means for transmitting the already discovered and the already "known."

Societies in which most or all of these conditions are found are, it seems to us, more likely to have a high rate of creativity than those in which they are not found.

The reverse also may be true. "If society sinks into the absolute rut of custom, if it refuses to accept beneficial mutations in the cultural realm," says Loren Eiseley, "or to tolerate, if not promote, the life of genius, then its unwieldy slumbers may be its last."

Archaeology is constantly digging up the remains of societies like that.

In fact, there appears to be enough known about the necessary social conditions for creativity that we can predict, with reasonable accuracy, the kind of innovations that are likely to be produced.

"Can we," asks Harold D. Lasswell in *The Social Setting of Creativity,* "improve our anticipation and understanding of innovation by analyzing all the significant contours to be found in a given social context as a whole, or in selected situations within it? If we locate the contours we may even predict that the corresponding innovations will be made by several individuals at the same time . . .

"By considering in advance a range of environmental changes, can we predict innovations? . . . If we are successful, it should be possible to locate the centers, routes and zones where innovations of a given kind will occur."

It seems quite possible that, in the near future, properly programmed computers may well be able to construct models of creativity for the societies in which they function and that the prediction of creativity may become a creative act itself. One would assume that prediction would be accompanied or followed by search and reward systems.

If, and when, this happens, we may have something that was foreshadowed by nature long ago, when it set upon the organizing ability of organisms as the expression of life—a truly and deliberately creative society in which each individual is able to enjoy the fullest development of his abilities, whatever they may be.

> Old Bureaucrat, my comrade, it is not you who are to blame. No one ever helped you to escape. You, like the termite, built your peace by blocking up with cement every chink and cranny through which the light might pierce. You rolled yourself up into a ball in your genteel security, in routine, in the stifling convention of provincial life, raising a modest rampart against the winds and the tides and the stars. You have chosen not to be perturbed by our great problems, have trouble enough to forget your faith as a man. You are not a dweller upon an errant planet and do not ask yourself questions to which there are no answers . . . Nobody grasped you by the shoulder while there was still time. Now the clay of which you were shaped has dried and hardened, and not in you will ever awaken the sleeping musician, the poet, the astronomer that possibly inhabited you from the beginning.
>
> —Antoine de Saint-Exupéry
> *"Wind, Sand and Stars"*

> The reciprocal relationship between culture and creativity is such that a creative product is not really an invention unless it is socially accepted. The creative product has to operate within the culture; it has to work. If it does not work, it is a failure as an invention.
>
> —Morton I. Teicher
> *"Culture and Creativity"*

> Perhaps if we were franker on personal creativity, we might reach out and occasionally touch, with a passing radiance, some other star in the night.
>
> —Loren Eiseley
> *"The Mind as Nature"*

Work in the Secular City

Harvey Cox

For all intents and purposes, we live in a secularized and urbanized age. Our domain is no longer the sacred community that our grandparents lived in, isolated, self-sufficient, rural, homespun, sentimental. Theologian Harvey Cox has shocked the American public a number of times, but the shocks go deep in his fine book, *The Secular City*. In this selection, he describes the place of work in that world.

The twin tendencies of urbanization and secularization have an enormous impact on work. We shall restrict ourselves in this chapter to three basic alterations they produce: . . .

The Separation of Places of Work and Residence

Several trends in technopolitan society tend to separate the place one works from the place one resides. The growing specialization of work demands that those with comparable specialties gather in more and more highly concentrated areas. The laws of efficiency, which point in most instances toward increased size, have with minor exceptions killed off the family farm and the small family business. . . .

The net result is that the workplace, the marketplace, and the school have moved away from residential areas. The butchers and grocers have set themselves up behind glittering glass-and-steel showcases of shopping centers surrounded by endless acres of parking lots. Shoe salesmen, druggists, clothing and hardware dealers are following suit quickly. The Fuller brush man still rings the doorbell, as does the junior high student selling magazines. But most of the selling now goes on in the vast emporia of our air-conditioned bazaars. Other activities are showing the same tendency. Schools are placed in specially demarcated

Reprinted with permission of the author and The Macmillan Company from *The Secular City* by Harvey Cox. © Copyright Harvey G. Cox, 1965. From pp. 145–166, selected.

areas and consolidated into larger units. This is dictated by road safety and educational philosophy—and also by economics. . . .

. . . The account executive's long commutation to the suburbs or short trip to a high-rise apartment has a psychological as well as a logistical significance. During the time he tries to put behind him, at least in part, all the open questions he has left and concentrate on connecting his new woofer. The commuter-train tracks or the thruway connect his work with his home, but they also separate two sets of relationships which he feels are probably best kept somewhat apart. . . .

The Bureaucratic Organization of Work

The secularization of work has produced the organization, and with it something called the "Organization Man."

We must first realize that the organization is here to stay. There is simply no other way to run a world brimming with three billion people in the midst of an industrial epoch. Unless a nuclear war returns us to the culture of hunting and gathering tribes, our world will be increasingly organized as the decades go by. If we choose to live responsibly in the world, then we must face the issue of how we can harness organizational power for authentic human purposes.

We are right in refusing to allow organizations to identify persons completely with the functions they perform. As individuals we do well to develop a degree of "technological asceticism," a discipline that will prevent our becoming captives of our gadgets. But we should never make the mistake of identifying this personal stance with the wishful thinking that hankers after Walden Pond. . . .

As one aspect of secularization, the organization principle derives in part from the impact of the biblical faith on Western culture. This point is well argued by the German sociologist Dietrich Von Oppen.[1] He insists that in order to understand the "organization" we should compare it to the "order," the integrative principle it has replaced in Western society. The difference is crucial. The order had a traditional, ethnic, or sacral basis. The medieval guild, the Gothic tribe, the Greek polis,

---

1. Dietrich Von Oppen, *Die Personale Zeitalter* (Stuttgart: Verlags gemeinschaft Burkharatahaus und Kreuz-Verlag GMBH, 1960).

the primitive clan are examples of orders. An order encompasses all or most of the facets of social existence. It relates a person to a mythical past, a total way of life, a secure identity. It corresponds roughly to certain aspects of what we have designated as tribal and town society. In contrast to the order, the organization is flexible, future-oriented, secularized, and limited in its scope. . . .

Where the organization principle obtains, the members are assumed to be free and responsible persons with other more definitive relationships. Only the fanatic defines his existence in terms of his membership in any organization. It serves one purpose among many and he expects it to stay in its place. In return, the organization helps the person achieve some desired end, but does not seek to endow him with a total identity or life meaning. . . .

Our task in the age of organization is the recognition and responsible use of power. The frequent question, "How can I preserve my own individual values in a giant organization?" may be falsely put. From the biblical perspective, the first question is never "How can I save my own soul, skin, values, or personality?" Man is summoned to be concerned, first of all, for his neighbor. In the age of organization he can only do this by getting into the fray, by losing a little skin from his own nose, perhaps even a spiritual value here and there, in the tough but epochal battle for the control of the organization. But as he does leap in, perhaps at the risk of his own life, he may discover that, even in the age of organization, precisely he who loses his life gains it.

The Emancipation of Work from Religion

Secularization signifies the emancipation of man first from religious and then from metaphysical control. We have shown by comparing societies and institutions how this proceeds at different speeds on different levels of a society. In the Western world, human work presents a striking example of how we allow residual religious meanings to cling to an activity long after its authentic function has been secularized. We prove this by equating work with a job, a paid position supplied by the market. Even in technopolitan culture we still often hold to the proposition that having some kind of job is an indispensable character-building activity and perhaps even an act of religious devotion. . . .

This at least is the official ideology. Exceptions are made. People who inherit great wealth or live on income from investments are excepted. The blind and the sick, those physically unable to work, are usually not permitted to starve. But in most cases, the indispensable link between production and distribution is the job, and he who has no job does not participate in the economy. The system works comparatively well in a society where the market requires enough, or nearly enough, jobs to go around. But it fails catastrophically when the number of salable jobs is fewer than the number of people who need to be linked to the distributive economy. This is why we have a crisis of work in the United States today. There is lots of work to do but not enough jobs to go around. Then why should we not modify the system to cohere with the new social reality? After all, the job system is a rather arbitrary one. The job has not played this decisive a role in all societies.

The reason we feel unable to explore other ways of linking production to consumption is the religious meaning we still attach to the job. . . .

For the man who has left behind the tribal cultus but has not yet reached the stage of full secularity, the job has become a spiritual devotion. Its holy mysteries infect everything it touches and the intense attitudes created make reasonable adjustments in the economy exceedingly difficult. Max Weber saw this as early as 1904, when he wrote:

> Today the spirit of religious asceticism . . . has escaped from the cage . . . and the idea of duty in one's calling prowls about in our lives like the ghost of dead religious beliefs.[2]

. . . These attitudes are carried over from the period of the bourgeois town.

The conflict between work actualities and work attitudes is one of the clearest examples of the differential pace of secularization. We have in technopolis the technical and social basis for the emancipation of work. We could transform it from a drudgery into a delight. Yet we still cling to pious attitudes about work, predispositions inherited from a different era. But we shall eventually have to lay aside this idol too. Technopolis demands a new definition of work. Why?

The answer is the word *cybernation*. The word is a neologism that refers to the coupling of two previously discrete tendencies in technological society. The first is automation, the wholly mechanical operation of production machines; the second is cybernetics, the science of con-

---

2. Max Weber, *The Protestant Ethic and the Spirit of Capitalism* (New York: Charles Scribner's Sons, 1958), p. 192.

trol and feedback systems, especially in electronic computers. Cybernation means the hitching of the computer to the machine. It reduces the human role to programming the task and maintaining the equipment.

The introduction of cybernation has been called the "second industrial revolution," and it has caught up to us before we have really learned to deal with the first one. It will have an enormous impact on our society. First, there will be fewer jobs in the production sector; second, the jobs remaining will demand an ever-higher level of skills; but third, we shall be able for the first time to produce enough goods and services so that no person will need to live in poverty or deprivation. UN Secretary-General U Thant has described the revolutionary implications of this new reality in these terms:

> . . . the central stupendous truth about developed economies today is that they can have—in anything but the shortest run—the kind and scale of resources they decide to have. . . . It is no longer resources that limit decisions. It is the decision that makes the resources. This is the fundamental revolutionary change—perhaps the most revolutionary man has ever known.[3]

. . . The most serious obstacle standing between the present definition of work and the one we need, however, is not political. It is religious. It is the halo that work has inherited from the presecular epoch. Much of the almost ineradicable religious coloration of work has been perpetuated through a misunderstanding of the Protestant doctrine of vocation. It was popularly believed that this doctrine meant that God calls certain men to be butchers, others bakers, and still others to be candlestick makers. . . .

The call which comes to man from the Bible, the *vocatio,* summons him not to a job, but to joy and gratitude in whatever he is doing. It is equally relevant at work and at play—or in the "new leisure" in which work can become endowed with the quality of play. . . .

In a cybernated age, a productive job can no longer be the passport to participation in the economy. Everyone should receive an income and therefore access to the goods and services he needs merely because he is a human being. Work, freed from captivity to the market, is freed to become something very close to what today we call leisure—doing something because one wants to.

---

3. Quoted in Robert Theobold, "Need: A New Definition of Work," *New University Thought,* III (1963), p. 11.

The
Self
at Play

Man works. Why? Because he is in a pattern or tradition that says he must work. Freud (and indeed we, ourselves) often intimate that one of the truly meaningful ways of expressing and experiencing significant selfhood is through work. But man has enormous reserves of time and energy. Work and love aren't the only two avenues of expression. What of play? What of fun? What of humor, relaxation, laughter, enjoyment, creative meditation, and even non-particularly-creative doing-of-nothing?

Man is capable of and often surprisingly committed to an impressive amount of relaxation and play. This is as important a part of finding and expressing one's uniqueness, one's significance, as anything else we can do. Yet, our Puritan tradition, our Work-Sin Ethic, has made many of us afraid to have a good time. We feel work or school is only meaningful if it's laborious, tedious, and serious.

Unfortunately, this dichotomous way of thinking is so pervasive that we often think of "play" as the opposite of "work." To be truly holistic in our thinking and feeling, we should consider the division into *either* work or play as artificial as the division into good or bad, right or wrong, love or hate, beautiful or ugly, emotion or reason. Man is a total, integrated, holistic creature. Yet, his ways of thinking have trapped him into compartmentalized ways of thinking and understanding.

In the chapter to follow, we present two articles for your perusal. In the first, journalist-educator George B. Leonard describes the necessity of re-capturing the lost virture of ecstasy in one of our most important endeavors, education.

In the second article, Sidney Jourard, humanistic psychologist, tells us of our need for periods and places of creative "time out."

The Uses of Ecstasy

George B. Leonard

We are often such grim creatures. Certainly, life is often hard, and so is much of our labor, including our schooling. But is this all there is to our lives? Have we lost our sense of the ecstatic, the humorous, the fun? Humorists are forever telling us to learn (or re-learn) the art of enjoyment.

In this excerpt from his book, *Education and Ecstasy,* George B. Leonard, a journalist and educational consultant, tells us what we are missing by losing sight of our needs for ecstasy.

Unlimited amounts of power are coming into human hands, perhaps surpassing what even Huxley could have imagined a few short years ago. For example, the "breeder" reactors now under development promise to produce more nuclear fuel than they can use. Human control of the death rate already has set in motion a possibly catastrophic population rise, though the means for controlling the birth rate also are available. . . .

. . . It seems to demand a new kind of human being—one who is not driven by narrow competition, eager acquisition and aggression, but who spends his life in the joyful pursuit of learning. Such a human being, I feel, will result not so much through changed ideologies or economic systems as through changes in the process I have called "education.". . . .

As a chief ingredient in all this, as well as an alternative to the old reinforcers, I have named "ecstasy"—joy, *ananda,* the ultimate delight.

Our society knows little about this ingredient. In fact, every civilization in our direct lineage has tended to fear and shun it as a threat to reason and order. In a sense, they have been right. It is hard to imagine a more revolutionary statement for us than "The natural condition of the human organism is joy." For, if this is true, we are being daily cheated, and perhaps the social system that so ruthlessly steals our birthright *should* be overthrown. . . .

Perhaps it is time for scholars and pundits to engage in the serious study of delight. What are its dangers? What are its uses? I would suggest three primarily negative considerations as a beginning:

1. *Ecstasy is not necessarily opposed to reason.* On the other hand, it may help light the way toward relationships, societies, and educational systems in which reason and emotion are no longer at odds; in which, in fact, the two are so in tune that the terms themselves, as opposites, will atrophy.

2. *Ecstasy is not necessarily opposed to order.* On the other hand, it may help us redefine order. In the new definition, a balanced natural ecology in which all creatures grow and act freely represents order. . . . Life is an ordering force. Man is an ordering animal. Order will continue to evolve. Ecstasy is implicated in changing not the quantity, but the quality of order.

3. *Ecstasy is neither immoral nor moral in itself.* At times, forms of ecstasy have powered some of mankind's most destructive movements. The Third Reich, for example exhibited a certain ecstatic mania. But Hitler's "joy" was used to bolster the old reinforcement system—competition, acquisition, and aggression—carried to the most destructive extremes. It was not brought into play as an *alternative* reinforcement system designed to replace the old.

In dealing with ecstasy, as with all powerful forces, context is crucial. The context I have suggested is neither the wantonly Dionysian nor the purely contemplative, but the educational. Ecstasy is education's most powerful ally. It is reinforcer for and substance of the moment of learning.

Knowing this, the master teacher pursues delight. Even those best known as great lecturers have turned their lecture halls into theaters, shameless in their use of spells and enchantments. Great men, as every schoolboy knows, have greeted their moments of learning with crazy joy. We learn how Archimedes leaped, crying, "Eureka!" from his bathtub; how Handel, on finishing the "Hallelujah Chorus," told his servant, "I did think I did see all Heaven before me, and the great God himself"; how Nietzsche wrote *Thus Spake Zarathustra:*

> There is an ecstasy such that the immense strain of it is sometimes relaxed by a flood of tears, along with which one's steps either rush or involuntarily lag, alternately. There is the feeling that one is completely out of hand, with the very distinct consciousness of an endless number of fine thrills and quiverings to the very toes.

What we fail to acknowledge is that every child starts out as an Archimedes, a Handel, a Nietzsche. The eight-month-old who succeeds in balancing one block on another has made a connection no less momentous for him than Nietzsche's. He cannot verbalize it so eloquently and probably would not bother to if he could; such moments are not so rare for him as for Nietzsche. Much of his life at that age, in fact, is learning. The possibilities of an endless series of ecstatic moments stretches before him. We quell the ecstasy and the learning but this is hard work and rarely is it entirely successful. Explaining why he was unable to think about scientific problems for a year after his final exams, Albert Einstein said:

> It is in fact nothing short of a miracle that the modern methods of instruction have not yet entirely strangled the holy curiosity of inquiry. . . . It is a very grave mistake to think that the enjoyment of seeing and searching can be promoted by means of coercion and a sense of duty.

And yet, life and joy cannot be subdued. The blade of grass shatters the concrete. The spring flowers bloom in Hiroshima. An Einstein emerges from the European academies. Those who would reduce, control, quell must lose in the end. The ecstatic forces of life, growth and change are too numerous, too various, too tumultuous. . . .

Life has one ultimate message, "Yes!" repeated in infinite number and variety. Human life, channeled for millennia by Civilization, is only just beginning to express the diversity and range of which it is easily capable. To affirm, to follow ecstasy in learning—in spite of injustice, suffering, confusion and disappointment—is to move more easily toward an education, a society that would free the enormous potential of man. . . .

William Golding's novel of some years back, *Lord of the Flies*, generally has been interpreted as a bitter commentary on man's nature. In it, a group of children, marooned on a deserted island, turn from Ralph, the voice of Civilized reason, and Piggy, his myopic egghead sidekick, to join Jack, who has been interpreted as the villain, the savage, the dark spirit in man that invariably emerges when the Civilized restraints are removed.

But Golding stacked the deck in a way that comments more on Civilization than on "human nature." Ralph is "good," but dull, unimaginative and indecisive. Piggy has "mind," but not much else. He is physically and sensorially inept. Jack, on the other hand, is physically and mentally alert, resourceful, imaginative and creative. He encourages his followers in games and chants, colorful costumes and face paint, ceremonies and a sense of community. He organizes successful pig hunts and provides his meat-hungry children with torchlit feasts. Meanwhile, Ralph and his dispirited followers sicken on their unvarying diet of fruit. What child would not follow Jack? When Golding makes Jack's group evil, he reveals the usual inability in our time to equate the ecstatic with the good. When he makes Civilized Ralph dull and inept, he reveals what he really feels about Civilization as he knows it.

When men must serve as predictable, prefabricated components of a rigid social machine, the ecstatic is not particularly useful and may, in fact, erode the compartments so necessary for the machine's functioning. But when a society moves away from the mechanistic, when an individual may function as a free-roving seeker, when what we now term "leisure" occupies most of an individual's hours, ecstasy may usefully accompany almost every act. Technology is preparing a world in which we may be learners all life long. In this world, delight will not be a luxury but a necessity.

I can recall little of what happened in school the winter I was fifteen. Perhaps that was the year everyone in my English class had to do a chapter-by-chapter synopsis of *Treasure Island*. But the afternoons and nights of that period still are vivid. I was infected by the ham radio bug. My next-door neighbor, a boy two years older, had got me started, and I lived for months in a state of delicious excitement. I would rush home from school, knowing the day would not be long enough. I would work steadily, practicing code, devouring ham manuals and magazines, poring over catalogues of radio parts, building simple shortwave receivers. I loved everything about it. When later I read Gerard Manley Hopkins' "Pied Beauty," the phrase, "all trades, their gear and tackle and trim," immediately summoned up the coils and condensers, the softly glowing vacuum tubes, the sizzle and smell of hot solder, the shining curls of metal drilled out of a chassis.

One night, my radio experience came to a moment of climax. For weeks I had been working on my first major effort, a four-tube regenerative shortwave receiver. The design was "my own," derived from circuits in the manuals and approved by my knowledgeable friends. Every part was of the highest quality, all housed in a professional-looking black metal cabinet. Every knob and dial was carefully positioned for efficiency and esthetics, and there was an oversized, freewheeling band-spread tuning knob. That particular night I had been working ever since running most of the way home from school. I had skipped dinner, fiercely overriding my parents' protests. And now, at about eleven o'clock, I soldered the last connection.

With trembling hands, I connected the ground and the antenna, plugged in the socket and switched on the set. There was a low, reassuring hum and, after a suspenseful wait, the four tubes lit up. I increased the volume. Dead silence. Nothing. I checked all the switches and dials. No problem there. Perhaps it was the speaker. I plugged in the earphones. Still nothing.

I couldn't imagine what was the matter. For the next hour or so, I went over every connection, traced the circuit until I was dizzy. Since I had splurged on all-new parts, I didn't even consider that one of them might be defective. The mystery, so powerful and unfathomable, could obviously have been cleared up in a few minutes by any well-equipped radio repairman. But, for me, its unraveling was momentous.

The radio's circuit consisted of two stages. The first stage converted radio frequency waves to electrical impulses of an audible frequency; the second stage served as an amplifier for the electrical impulses coming from the first stage. I hit upon the idea of tapping the earphones in at the end of the first stage. Success! Static, code, voices. This seemed to indicate to me that the trouble lay somewhere in the second stage. On an impulse, however, I tied in a microphone at the very beginning of the second stage. Success again. The second stage worked. I could hear my voice coming from the speaker.

At that very instant, the answer was clear: Both stages worked separately. The trouble had to lie in the coupling between them. My eyes went to a little green and silver coil *(the broken connection between subconscious and conscious, the hidden flaw between individual and community)*. It *had* to be that impedance coil. With this certainty, I was quite overcome. I would gladly have broken into a radio store to get another one, but my friend, I found, had a spare. I tied it in, not bothering for the moment to solder it. And a universe poured into my room from the star-filled night. I spun the dial: a ham in Louisiana, in California; shortwave broadcasts from England, Germany, Mexico, Brazil. There was no end to it. I had put out new sensors. Where there had been nothing, there was *all of this*.

Ecstasy is one of the trickier conditions to write about. But if there is such a thing as being transported, I was transported that night. And I was, as with every true learning experience, forever afterwards changed.

Society's Need for Respectable "Check-Out Places"

Sidney M. Jourard

Schoolchildren aren't expected to spend the entire day at their desks, heads buried in their books. We have, in this enlightened age, seen fit to space their workday with recess periods, time when they can exercise their bodies as they also do their brains. In most businesses, lunch and coffee breaks are now a regular part of the workday. Most of us also have vacation periods, giving us a break in the routine.

Sidney Jourard proposes a further step: periods of "time out" with special places to go. Jourard is not just fantasizing; he is serious in his intent. People need opportunities for re-creation. In the following excerpt from *Disclosing Man to Himself,* he spells out for us how his theory would work and with what benefits.

A person needs a place to go when he finds his life unlivable. Society seems to conspire such that there is nowhere to go when you want to be offstage, free from your usual roles, free to discover and define your being-for-yourself. Judges, critics, and commissars are omnipresent. If a man steps out of line and departs from his usual roles, someone is there to remind him of who he is, to define him, and to punish him for daring to define himself. The upshot is many wives and mothers find they cannot face their families another moment without shrieking in protest against the sameness of their unappreciated daily grind. But they stifle the shriek and carry on. Fathers and husbands become bored with their wives, infuriated by their children, and worn out by work that lacks joy—continued only because there is no other work to do, and the bills fall due each month. The children, in turn, cannot get along with each other, or with their parents. Grandparents, aunts, and uncles live a thousand miles away and cannot take the youngsters in for a week or month of respite. And so the trapped ones persist on their joyless, desperate treadmills until physical illness grants them a ticket of admission to a hospital or sickroom. Or they "blow up," have a nervous breakdown, and are treated as "not in their right minds." They may enter a mental hospital, there to be placed in storage until the regime of shock, tranquilizers, and periodic consultations with an overworked psychiatrist brings them "to their senses." But even in the hospitals, there is no respite from roles; patients are cast into new ones and lack the freedom to choose their being. They return to the way of life they lived before, perhaps with the protest in them electroshocked or drugged out of existence.

Before this drama reaches its climax in the sickroom or the state hospital, it would be helpful if new alternatives could be provided. What would life in our society be like if we had acceptable "check-out places"? In moments of reverie, I have invented some. Let me describe one such, a healing-house that appeals to me. It is probably healing only for middle-class people.

It is a place where one can enter and find confirmation for *any* way one has chosen to be, or any way that circumstances have brought one to. If a man wishes solitude, he can find it there; and no one will speak to him if he wishes to remain silent. If he wishes congenial and enlivening body-contact, a masseur or masseuse (he can choose which) is available to provide service. If a housewife wants to paint, listen to music, or just sit and meditate, there is a room for her to do so. The place would be like the now outdated retreats and monasteries that once were available for the defeated and the sick in spirit.

Each person would be entitled to a cell with inviolate privacy. There he could go, and stay for a day, a week, a month, or years. No one could enter this little womb without his invitation; and once a person closed the door, no one else could enter.

Routine would be simple and minimal in such a haven. Meals would be spartan. A person could take them communally, in the dining hall, if he wished to socialize, and take part in the preparation and clean-up from the repast. Otherwise, the pantry would be always available, with abundant supplies of fruit, bread, milk, raw vegetables, and similar snacks. A resident could come and go, nibbling as he wished.

If he wished conversation, he could go to the common room, where he could sit; and his presence alone would signify that he would be willing to talk. Or he could invite someone to the privacy of his cell, if he wished to enter into uninterrupted dialogue.

The rule of the house would be freedom for the self, with respect for the freedom of the other.

People who entered would leave their roles at the doorstep. No status, no rank, would interpose itself between the guests—who would have a first name, or a surname, or no name, or a pseudonym, if that was what they chose.

This would be a place where people could quite freely go out of their minds and roles, as these were known outside.

The house would not be solely for those harried, middle-class people who needed a place to go before they broke down. It would also be a place where creative people—writers, painters, dancers, poets—could go to live awhile and present their more tender creations in an accepting, or better, honest milieu, where commercial criteria for judging art and ideas are irrelevant.

This would be a place where one could go to redefine himself, apart from the people "back home," who have a vested interest in keeping the person in the roles by which they knew him, but which were sickening him. The fat ones could slim down, the thin ones increase in girth. The tense and nervous could find surcease and relaxation; the aimless might meet people with aims that could inspire and redirect their lives.

These houses would be the place one went *before* he got sick, or mad. The directors would eschew drugs and medicines. They would heal by letting healing take place. The houses would be places where joy could be experienced, and peace.

These islands or oases could exist in every community. The Howard Johnson- or Holiday Inn-builders could design them cheaply and simply enough—but with more taste, I would hope, than is shown in those rooms designed for everyone and hence no one. The staff of permanent residents could include professional psychotherapists, resident artists, playwrights, dancers, masseurs, writers and teachers, and musicians. Some of these residents might come and go; but all would provide seekers with an atmosphere of spiritual freedom, and examples of the quest for new avenues of being and expression. A workman, professional man, wife or mother, or lonely person could come daily for an hour or so, or weekly, and find relaxation, edification, or companionship. Americanized versions of geisha girls, or geisha men, would be available, not for illicit and illegal prostitution, but for the purpose of inviting a person into the dialogue that leads a man beyond his usual consciousness, even to delight.

I have little doubt that such houses would pay for themselves if they were on a private, pay-as-you-go basis. And I suspect that if they were underwritten by some grant, or by public-health moneys—but with their operation strictly in the hands of the director of each house—they would more than pay for themselves, in the form of physical breakdown that did *not* happen and mental breakdown which would *not* materialize. I suspect that for the people who patronized such a house, intake of drugs and medicines would diminish radically, to the dismay of the pharmaceutical houses. The mass invasion of physicians' clinics and waiting-rooms would be reduced to manageable dimensions. And the waiting lists of practicing psychotherapists would doubtless be less packed with names.

Such houses of retreat and healing will, alas, not become part of every village, town, or city neighborhood. But sensible people will find ways to pool resources so that they can organize them by themselves. Or if they can afford it, they will buy or rent a "pad" on the other side of town, away from family and friends. Perhaps some organizational genius will find the necessary staff, and the capital to invest; and he will become a millionaire by providing what everyone needs, at a price all can afford to pay.

If such places came into being as a normal part of society, I suspect psychotherapists would lose some of their present *raison d'être,* and would have to apply their knowledge of how people sicken and become whole to teaching, and to living fulfilled lives themselves, so that by their being, they would represent viable ways. And I suspect that physicians would find their practices confined to delivering babies, setting broken bones, and stanching the flow of blood. Sales of drugs would diminish, and the directors of pharmaceutical firms would send lobbies to Washington to persuade legislators the houses were subversive and un-American.

8

Masking
and
Unmasking

In the process of living, we do many interesting things. Among them are the roles and games we play with ourselves and others. In this section we want to look at how putting on of masks, either by ourselves or by others, hinders the self-actualization process. Traditionally, there have been groups in our society that have had to wear the masks and play the roles assigned to them by others. This is usually because the majority—or the ones in power— have only been able to go on being in the majority or in power by having these others play specific roles. A person is more than any one mask. But we all know that some people can show only those parts of their identity that they think are safe, that they know will be accepted.

Recently, we have seen new identities emerging in America. We refer to those who have thrown aside the mask that they've been forced or expected to wear. They now stand before us unhidden and open, not asking, but demanding to be seen, known, and acknowledged. We don't always like such people—not because they are necessarily bad, wrong, unpleasant, or dangerous, but because they upset our expectations about them. We refer, of course, to the women in various liberation movements, who are insisting that women are not *things,* but full, free persons. We refer, also, to those in various minority groups, who refuse to play the mask game any longer. Negroes, preferring the term "blacks," are saying that white America can have its "Nigger Masks" back; they aren't needed anymore. Young people are also discarding the masks given them by parents and teachers in particular, by society in general. They are showing in many ways that they are full-fledged persons, though many people don't like all the methods used, especially by college students.

It's an interesting commentary that people who refuse to wear the expected masks are labelled "militant," "radical," "revolutionary." Some are, of course. But, the majority impress us as simply people who are discovering some of the pleasures of significant selfhood.

In the first article of this chapter, James F. T. Bugental, a psychologist and pioneer in the Humanistic movement, describes some of the reasons people wear masks.

In the second, Robert Penn Warren, an eminent writer of many insightful pieces of literature, describes one of the great un-maskers of our day, Malcolm X. Malcolm X has become a representative of the New Black who has set out his real identity for all of us to see.

The Forfeiting of Authenticity

James F. T. Bugental

Why do we mask our authentic selves? Why do we deny ourselves the fulfillment of our significant potential? Is it only our fear, or is it ignorance of the better possibilities we possess? James F. T. Bugental believes that much of our masking—of our hiding from authentic Being—is felt to be necessary for survival. Authentic Being (another way of saying Significant Selfhood) is a frightening thing, especially if you're not used to it. See if in reading this you discover some of your own self-blackmail coming to light.

From Chapter 3, from *The Search for Authenticity* by J. F. T. Bugental. Copyright © 1965 by Holt, Rinehart and Winston, Inc. Reprinted by permission of Holt, Rinehart and Winston, Inc.

Each of us is like a person who pays blackmail to keep a feared reality from becoming manifest. So paying, we maintain a semblance of peace at increasingly heavy cost to our resources. By our very nature, we seek to actualize ourselves in the world. It follows that the threat from which we pull away, against which we erect our constricting distortions of reality, is the threat of non-being, of the non-actuality of ourselves. The paying of blackmail, then, is the trading-off of some of our actuality-of-being-in-the-world to hold off non-being. But, of course, to the extent that we so trade our actuality, we are in that measure non-actual. This is the joker in the transaction. This is the existential meaning of the race-old legend of selling one's soul to the devil (stories that usually included the devil's gift somehow betraying the buyer). When we seek to evade the anxieties of being authentic, we lose our being and incur renewed, neurotic anxiety.

We may cast this whole process into a paraphrase that will illustrate the "Waking Nightmare of Neurosis."

> I am thrown into world without instruction. Each action I take or do not take is fraught with possibility. Possibility extends on all sides through all dimensions from life to death, from good to evil, from fulfilling to negating. And I do not know. I do not know enough; I do not know what may happen; I cannot be sure of any consequences. And so I am afraid. I cannot ask, for none can tell me. I cannot study, for none can teach. What I have done and what I have not done weigh on me. What I will yet do or will not do threaten me. And yet I will be; and being, I will do and not do. And doing, I will be the doer and responsible for having done. And not doing, I will be the not-doer and responsible for not having done.

This is Man's autobiography. But yet, he writes another chapter. This chapter shows the impact of anxiety.

> I am afraid. I cannot endure not knowing. It is too much to be responsible for what I cannot control. I am so alone, so unprotected.

Then, man may write still another chapter:

> The world is really not so unknowable. If I but keep my eyes from seeing too much, my ears from hearing too much, my mind from thinking too much, it becomes quite reasonable. I can even persuade myself I see all there is. If I but worship this deity, adhere to this virtue, suffer that pain, insist on that plan, world becomes quite manageable.

If I but hush the voice of possibility both within and about me, the fear grows quieter, I am no longer afraid, so much.[1]

Many, if not all, therapeutic systems can have favorable results because they provide the medium, the therapeutic relation, that encourages the confronting and discarding of self-and-world distortions that are no longer functionally required. However, many therapists (and therapeutic systems) seem to stop there, others seem content to act like parents "writing an excuse" to a teacher for the patient so he can (apparently) avoid contingency-responsibility-tragedy: "Please excuse Mr. Smith from contingency. He had bad parents."

We cannot comprehend ourselves-and-world. But this at once provides no excuse from responsibility in the world and yet prevents that responsibility being devastating. Could we know fully (comprehend) we would have no choice, no being. Were we not responsible, we would be meaningless, fluff on a vagrant breeze. The beauty and the terror of our plight is to be responsible without being able to know enough to discharge our responsibility perfectly.[2]

We seek to increase our authenticity (therapy seeks to free the patient of the ways he forestalls his own authenticity). I say "increase" because authenticity is not a perfect state to be achieved but a quantitative dimension along which we can move. When I spoke of paying blackmail, I meant trading off authenticity for seeming security.

What are the attributes of being authentic?

1. Being as fully aware as I can be at the moment.
2. Choosing what possibility I will invest with my life, with actuality, at the moment.
3. Taking responsibility for the choice I have made while yet recognizing the imperfection of my awareness and the fact that my choice gave this alternative actuality and not some other. Recognizing therein that tragedy is always potential and that neither my limitations of awareness, nor my good intentions, nor my suffering, nor my virtue, nor any other extrinsic circumstance, can change that fact.

1. Bugental, J. F. T., "Self-Fragmentation as a Resistance to Self-Actualization," *Review of Existential Psychology and Psychiatry*, Vol. 2 (1962), pp. 241–248.
2. Maslow, A. H., *Summer Notes . . .* (Del Mar, Calif., Non-Linear Systems, Inc., 1962).

Our patients (and we) seek to be excused from this awful actuality. We want to play "not for keeps," to have it "not count," to say "slips go over."

We fear the Godlike weight of giving life and administering death to possibilities. We want to hide under the bed clothes from the shadowy Could-have-been and the relentless Is.

> For of all sad words of tongue or pen,
> The saddest are these: 'It might have been!'

And I am the one who decided it would not be.

Malcolm X

Robert Penn Warren

Who was Malcolm X? A hateful racial extremist? A saint for our times? His *Autobiography* gave us a chance to see the process by which Malcolm Little gradually learned to outgrow his mask of subservient, outlawed "niggerhood," and discover his own identity as a black man. In this article, Robert Penn Warren, a Southern writer of great talent, examines some of Malcolm's traits, against his background and his involvement with the Muslim Movement.

Though many black people today disavow any connection with the Muslims or Malcolm X, he definitely stands as one of the folk-heroes of the new black-consciousness community.

James Farmer, lately the National Director of the Committee of Racial Equality, has called Malcolm X a "very simple man." Elijah Poole, better known to the Black Muslims as Muhammad and, indeed, as Allah, called him a "star gone astray." An editorial writer of the

From Malcolm X: Mission and Meaning, by Robert Penn Warren. Reprinted by permission of William Morris Agency, Inc., on behalf of author. Copyright © 1967 by Robert Penn Warren.

Saturday Evening Post put it: "If Malcolm X were not a Negro, his autobiography would be little more than a journal of abnormal psychology, the story of a burglar, dope pusher, addict and jailbird—with a family history of insanity—who acquires messianic delusions and sets forth to preach an upside-down religion of 'brotherly' hatred." Carl Rowan, a Negro, lately the director of the United States Information Service, substantially agreed with that editorial writer when he said, in an interview after Malcolm's assassination, that he was "an ex-convict, ex-dope peddler who became a racial fanatic." Another editorial writer, that of the *Daily Times* of Lagos, Nigeria, called him a martyr.

Malcolm X may have been, in varying perspectives, all these things. But he was also something else. He was a latter-day example of an old-fashioned type of American celebrated in grammar school readers, commencement addresses, and speeches at Rotary Club lunches—the man who "makes it," the man who, from humble origins and with meager education, converts, by will, intelligence, and sterling character, his liabilities into assets. Malcolm X was of that breed of Americans, autodidacts and homemade successes, that has included Benjamin Franklin, Abraham Lincoln, P. T. Barnum, Charles A. Edison, Booker T. Washington, Mark Twain, Henry Ford, and the Wright brothers. Malcolm X would look back on his beginnings and, in innocent joy, marvel at the distance he had come.

But in Malcolm X the old Horatio Alger story is crossed, as has often been the case, with another typical American story. America has been prodigally fruitful of hot-gospellers and prophets—from Dr. Graham and his bread, Amelia Bloomer and her bloomers, Emerson and the Oversoul, and Brigham Young, on to F.D.R. and the current Graham, Billy. Furthermore, to round out his American story and insure his fame, Malcolm X, like John Brown, Abraham Lincoln, Joseph Smith (the founder of Mormonism), and John Fitzgerald Kennedy, along with a host of lesser prophets, crowned his mission with martyrdom. Malcolm X fulfills, it would seem, all the requirements—success against odds, the role of prophet, and martyrdom—for inclusion in the American pantheon.

Malcolm Little, who was to become Malcolm X and El-Hajj Malik El-Shabazz, was born in Omaha, Nebraska, on May 19, 1925. All omens were right, and all his background. He was the seventh child of his father. One night during the pregnancy of his mother, hooded Ku Klux Klansmen, mounted and brandishing rifles and shotguns, surrounded the house, calling for the father to come out; the mother faced them down and persuaded them of the fact that her husband was not at home. The mother, a West Indian who looked white, was ashamed, not proud, of the white blood. The father, a Baptist preacher, was a militant follower of Marcus Garvey, and this was to lead to another attack on the Little home, in 1929, in Lansing, Michigan, this time by the Black Legion, which except for black robes was indistinguishable from the Klan; the house burned to the ground, while white police and firemen looked on. The memory of that night stayed with Malcolm from childhood—that and the pictures his father showed him of Marcus Garvey "riding in a fine car, a big black man dressed in a dazzling uniform with gold braid on it, and he was wearing a thrilling hat with tall plumes," and the Garveyite meetings at which his father presided and which always ended with the exhortation, "Up, you mighty race, you can accomplish what you will!" The people would chant these words after Malcolm's father.

To complete the picture of the preparation of the hero for his mission, his father, who had seen two brothers killed by white men and a third lynched, was found, one night, on a streetcar track, with skull crushed and body cut almost across. Negroes in Lansing —and the son all his life—believed that he had been attacked by white men, and then laid on the track. Malcolm always believed that he, too, would meet a violent death. When he first became aware of the long stalk, which was to end in gunfire in the Audubon Ballroom, Malcolm might accept it, then, as a fulfillment of old omens and intuitions.

In spite of the powerful image of the father, the pictures of Garvey in uniform, and the tales of black kings, Malcolm's early notion of Africa was still one "of naked savages, cannibals, monkeys and tigers and steaming jungles." He says that he never understood why. But that statement must be an example, in a form more bland than usual, of his irony, for a large part of his autobiography (*The Autobiography of Malcolm X,* with the assistance of Alex Haley, New York City: The Grove Press, 1966) is devoted to explaining *why*—that is, by the white man's "brain-washing"; and then explaining *how*, step by step, he came to the vision of another Africa, and of another self, different from the hustler, pimp, dope-addict, dope-pusher, burglar, and, by his own account, generally degraded and vice-ridden creature known as "Satan," who, in 1948, in Concord Prison, in Massachusetts, heard, in a letter from his brother Philbert, of the "natural religion for the black man." The religion was called the "Nation of Islam."

This autobiography is "told" to Alex Haley, a Negro, a retired twenty-year man of the Coast Guard turned journalist. From 1963 up to the assassination, Haley saw Malcolm for almost daily sessions when Malcolm was in New York, and sometimes accompanied him on his trips. Haley's account of this period, of how he slowly gained Malcolm's confidence and how Malcolm himself discovered the need to tell his story, is extremely interesting and, though presented as an Epilogue, is an integral part of the book; but the main narrative has the advantage of Malcolm's tone, his characteristic movement of mind, and his wit, for Haley has succeeded admirably in capturing these qualities, as can be checked by the recollection of Malcolm's TV appearances and conversation and by his taped speeches (*Malcolm X Speaks: Selected Speeches and Statements,* edited by George Breitman, New York: Merit Publishers, 1966).

The *Autobiography* and the speeches are an extraordinary record of an extraordinary man. They are, among other things, a record that may show a white man (or some Negroes, for Malcolm would say that many Negroes do not know the nature of their own experience) what it means to be a Negro in America, in this century, or at least what it so dramatically meant to one man of unusual intelligence and powerful personality. Being a Negro meant being "black"—even if black was no more than a metaphor for Malcolm, who was himself "marginy," a dull yellowish skin, pale enough to freckle, pale eyes, hair reddish-coppery. He had been "Detroit Red" in his hustling days.

To be black, metaphorically or literally, meant, according to Malcolm, to wear a badge of shame which was so mystically and deeply accepted that all the practical injustices the white world might visit upon the black would seem only a kind of inverted justice, necessary in the very nature of things, the working out of a curse. The black man had no history, no country, no identity; he was alienated in time and place; he lived in "self-hate," and being unable to accept "self," he therefore was willing to accept, supine or with random violence, his fate. This was the diagnosis of his own plight, as Malcolm learned it from the "Nation of Islam."

As for the cure, what he found was the doctrine of the Black Muslims. This involved a history of creation and a metaphysic which made the black man central and dominant, and a secular history of kingly achievement in Africa. The divine and secular histories provided a justification for the acceptance of the black "self." In addition, the doctrine provided an understanding of the iniquity of the white man which would account for the black man's present lot and would, at the same time, mobilize an unquenchable hate against him. Total withdrawal from the white man and all his works was the path to virtue, until the day of Armageddon when he would be destroyed. Meanwhile, until the Chosen People had been relieved of the white man's presence, the black man was presented with a practical program of life: thrift, education, cleanliness, diet (no pork, for example, pork being a "nigger" food), abstemiousness (no alcohol or tobacco), manners and courtesy, puritanical morality and reverence for the home and Muslim womanhood— a general program of "wake up, clean up, and stand up." In fact, on the practical side, in spite of the hatred of the white man and contempt for his culture, the Black Muslim doctrine smuggled into the life of the Negro slum the very virtues which had made white middle-class America what it was—i.e., successful.

After Malcolm's death Dr. Kenneth B. Clark, the Negro psychologist and the author of an important book called *Dark Ghetto,* said that he had been "cut down at the point when he seemed on the verge of achieving the position of respectability he sought." In the midst of the gospel of violence and the repudiation of the white world, even in the Black Muslim phase, there appears now and then the note of yearning. In the *Autobiography* we find, for instance, this passage: "I was the invited speaker at the Harvard Law School Forum. I happened to glance through a window. Abruptly, I realized that I was looking in the direction of the apartment house that was my old burglary group's hideout. . . . And there I stood, the invited speaker, at Harvard."

Malcolm, still in prison, gave up pork and tobacco, and undertook a program of reading in the good library there available. He read in Plato, Aristotle, Schopenhauer, Kant, Nietzsche, and the "Oriental philosophers." He read and reread the Bible, and could match quotations with a Harvard Seminary student who conducted a class for prisoners. He studied *The Loom of Language,* by Frederick Bodmer, and memorized Grimm's Law. He read Durant's *Story of Civilization,* H. G. Wells' *Outline of History,* Herodotus, Fannie Kimball, *Uncle Tom's Cabin,* Gandhi, Gregor Mendel, pamphlets of the "Abolitionist Anti-Slavery Society of New England," and J. A. Rogers' *Sex and Race.* He was trying to find the black man's place—and his own—in history, trying, in other words, to document the doctrine of the Black Muslims. He wrote regularly to Muhammad to tell what he had found. While he was still in prison Malcolm also had a vision. He had written an appeal to Muhammad to reinstate his brother Reginald, suspended as a Muslim for "improper relations" with the secretary of the New York Temple. That night he spent in desperate prayer. The next night he woke up and saw a man sitting, there in the cell, in a chair by him. "He had on a dark suit, I remember. I could see him as plainly as I see anyone I look at. He wasn't black, and he wasn't white. He was light-brown-skinned, an Asiatic cast of countenance, and he had oily black hair. . . . I had no idea whatsoever who he was. He just sat there. Then suddenly as he had come, he was gone." The color of the man in the vision is an interesting fact. So is his immobility and silence.

When Malcolm Little came out of prison, he was Malcolm X, the "X," according to the practice of the Black Muslims, standing for the true name lost long ago in Africa to take the place of the false white name that had been forced on him. He had been reborn, and he now entered upon his mission. Soon he was an accredited minister of Muhammad, the official defender of the faith and the intellectual spokesman of the movement. His success, and especially the fact that he was invited to colleges, where Muhammad would never be invited, led to jealousy and, as Malcolm reports, contributed to his "silencing" as soon as a good justification appeared.

Malcolm X was not the only man drawn from the lower depths to be reborn in the Nation of Islam. It is generally admitted that the record of rehabilitation by the Black Muslims of dope-addicts, alcoholics, prostitutes, and criminals makes any other method seem a waste of time. They have, it would seem, found the nerve center that, once touched, can radically change both the values and the way of life for a number of Negroes in America; and it is important here to use the phrase "Negroes in America" with special emphasis, and no other locution, for those redeemed by the Black Muslims are those who have been only *in*, but not *of*, America, those without country, history, or identity. The Black Muslims have found, then, a principle that, if not of universal validity (or, in one perspective, isn't it? for white as well as for black?), at least involves a truth of considerable psychological importance. That truth is, indeed, shrouded in metaphysical mumbo-jumbo, political and economic absurdity, and some murderous delusions, but even these elements have a noteworthy symbolic relation to the central truth. It is reported that Martin Luther King, after seeing Malcolm X on TV, remarked: "When he starts talking about all that's been done to us, I get a twinge of hate, of identification with him. But hate is not the only effect." A man as intelligent, as cultivated, and as experienced as James Farmer has testified in his recent book *Freedom When?* that the Black Muslims and Malcolm X have had a very important impact on his own thinking and in helping to change his basic views of the Negro Revolution, especially on the question of "blackness" and on the nature of integration and the Negro's role in an open society.

If this is the case, then the story of Malcolm X assumes an added dimension. It shows the reader the world in which that truth can operate; that is, it shows the kind of alienation to which this truth is applicable. It shows, also, the human quality of the operation, a man in the process of trying to understand his plight, and to find salvation, by that truth. But there is another aspect to the *Autobiography*. Malcolm X was a man in motion, he was a seeker, and that motion led, in the end, away from orthodox Black Muslim doctrine. The doctrine had been, he said, a straitjacket. He was now in the process of stripping away, perhaps unconsciously, the mumbo-jumbo, the absurdities, and the murderous delusions. He was trying, as it were, to locate the truth that had saved him, and divest it of the irrelevancies. In the end, he might have come to regard the religion that, after his break with the Black Muslims, he had found in Mecca as an irrelevancy, too. Certainly, just before his death he could say that his "philosophy" was still changing. Perhaps what Mecca gave him, for the time being at least, was the respectability, the authority, of the established thing. But he might have finally found that authority in himself, for he could speak as a man whose very existence was witness to what he said. Something of that purely personal authority comes through in these books.

Malcolm X had, in his last phase, lost the mystique of blackness so important to the Black Muslims; he had seen the blue-eyed and fair-haired pilgrims in Mecca. He was no longer a separatist in the absolute sense of the Black Muslims. He had become enough of an integrationist to say: "I believe in recognizing every human being as a human being . . . and when you are dealing with humanity as a family, there's no question of integration or intermarriage. It's just one human being marrying another human being or one human being living around with another human being." And just before his death he had made a down-payment on a house, in Long Island, in a largely Jewish neighborhood. He no longer saw the white man as the "white devil"—metaphysically evil; and he was ready, grudgingly, not optimistically, and with a note of threat, to grant that there was in America a chance, a last chance, for a "bloodless revolution." He was ready to work with other Negro organizations, even those which he had most derided, to try to find common ground and solutions at a practical level.

Certain ideas were, however, carried over from the Black Muslim days. The question of "identity" remained, and the question of race pride and personal self-respect divested of chauvinism, and with this the notion of "wake up, clean up, and stand up," the notion of self-reliance, self-improvement, self-discipline. If he could say such things, which smacked of the discredited philosophy of Booker T. Washington, and which few other Civil Rights leaders would dare to utter, it was because he did so in the context of his intransigence vis-à-vis the white world and his radical indictment of white society. Even in the last phase, even if he believed in "recognizing every human being as a human being," and no longer took the white man to be metaphysically evil, his indictment of white society was still radical; unless that society could really be regenerated, the chance for the "bloodless revolution" was gone.

This radical indictment leads to what may be the greatest significance of Malcolm X, his symbolic role. He was the black man who looked the white man in the eye and forgave nothing. If the white man had turned away, in shame or indifference, from the awful "forgiveness" of a Martin Luther King, he still had to face the unforgiveness, with its shattering effect on his accustomed view of himself and with the terrifying discovery, as Malcolm's rage brought his own rage forth, of the ultimate of which he himself would, under pressure, be capable. To put it another way, Malcolm X let the white man see what, from a certain perspective, he, his history, and his culture looked like. It was possible to say that that perspective was not the only one, that it did not give the whole truth about the white man, his history, and his culture, but it was not possible to say that the perspective did not carry a truth, a truth that was not less, but more, true for being seen from the angle of "Small's Paradise" in Harlem or of the bedroom to which "Detroit Red," the "steerer," brought the "Ivy League fathers" to be ministered to by the big black girl, whose body had been greased to make it look "shinier and blacker" and whose Amazonian hand held a small plaited whip.

On the afternoon of Sunday, February 21, 1965, at a meeting of his struggling new Organization of Afro-American Unity, in the Audubon Ballroom, on West 166th Street, in Harlem, Malcolm X rose to speak and uttered the ritual greeting, *"Asalaikum,* brothers and sisters!" He was immediately cut down by shotgun and revolver fire from assassins waiting in the front of the audience. At 3:30 at the Columbia-Presbyterian Hospital, he was pronounced dead. Three men—Talmadge Thayer, Norman 3X (Brown), and Thomas 15X (Johnson)—were arrested in the case and tried for first-degree murder. Thayer denied Black Muslim connections, but Thomas 15X was identified as a member and Norman 3X as a lieutenant in the "Fruit of Islam"—the bodyguards of Elijah Muhammad. After deliberating for twenty hours a jury found them guilty, and all three were given life sentences.

What would have been Malcolm's role had he lived? Perhaps as some Negro leaders said shortly before his death, he had no real organization, and did not have the talent to create one. Perhaps his being in motion was only, as some held, a result of confusion of mind, a groping that could not be trusted to bring results. Perhaps, as James Farmer had put it, Malcolm, for all his talk, was not an activist; he had managed all along to be out of harm's way whenever harm was brewing, and he was afraid of the time when he "would have to chirp or get off the perch."

But perhaps the new phase of the Negro Revolution, with the violence of the great city slums, might have given him his great chance. He might have, at last, found himself in action. He might have found himself committed to blind violence, but on the other hand he might have had the power to control and canalize action and do something to reduce the danger of the Revolution's degenerating into random revolt. For, in spite of all the gospel of intransigence, Malcolm had always had a governing idea of a constructive role for the Negro, some notion of a society. After all, he had personal force, as no one who ever spent as little as ten minutes with him would have doubted: charisma, to use the fashionable word, and that to a degree possessed by no other leader except Martin Luther King. And he had one great asset which Martin Luther King does not have: he was from the lower depths and possessed the authority of one who had both suffered and conquered the depths.

Whatever the future might have held for him had he lived, his actual role was an important one, and in one sense the importance lay in his

being rather than his *doing*. He was a man of passion, depth, and scale—
and his personal story is a moving one. There is the long struggle. There
is the sense of desperation and tightening entrapment as, in the last
days, Malcolm recognized the dilemma developing in his situation. The
"so-called moderate" Civil Rights leaders, he said, dodged him as "too
militant," and the "so-called militants" dodged him as "too moderate."
Haley reports that he once exclaimed "They won't let me turn the
corner! I'm caught in a trap!" For there is a trap in the story, a real and
lethal one. There is the gang of Black Muslims covering his every move
in the Statler Hilton at Los Angeles, the mysterious Negro men who tried
to get his room number at the Hilton in New York City, and the sinister
telephone call to his room in the hotel the morning of his death. There
is the bombing of his house, and his despairing anger when the event
was widely taken as a publicity stunt. There is his remark to Haley, as
he asked to read the manuscript of his book for a last, unnecessary time:
"I just want to read it one more time, because I don't expect to read it in
finished form"—wanting, as it were, to get a last sense of the shape of
his own life as he felt the trap closing. There is, as with a final accent of
pathos, the letter by his six-year-old daughter Attilah (named for the
Scourge of God), written just after his death: "Dear Daddy, I love you
so. O dear, O dear, I wish you wasn't dead." But entrapment and pathos
was not all. He had been bred to danger. When he stepped on the plat-
form that Sunday afternoon, in the face of odds which he had more
shrewdly estimated than anybody else, he had nerve, confidence, style.
He made his last gesture.

As one reads the *Autobiography,* one feels that, whatever the historical importance of Malcolm Little, his story has permanence, that it
has something of tragic intensity and meaning. One feels that it is an
American story bound to be remembered, to lurk in the background of
popular consciousness, to reappear some day in a novel, on the stage,
or on the screen. No—the right medium might be the ballad. Malcolm
was a figure out of the anonymous depth of the folk, and even now, in
a slum bedroom or in the shadowy corner of some bar, fingers may be
tentatively picking the box, and lips fumbling to frame the words that
will mean, long after our present problems are resolved and forgotten,
the final fame, and the final significance.

The Self in Conflict

Not all our enemies are outside of us trying to get in or get at us. In addition to masks we choose or have forced on us, each of us is continually struggling with a whole host of internal forces: negative attitudes, doubts fears, unfulfilled dreams, self-hatred, and contradictory expressions of selfhood.

Some of these enemies within produce only minor impasses in the Struggle for Significant Selfhood. Others produce more serious consequences, some of which hurt us very badly. Sometimes the conflict eats into the very being of an individual and he lives a crippled, partially-fulfilled existence. The latter situation is sometimes called "mental or emotional illness."

It's important to remember that some of these internalized conflicts are self-chosen and self-imposed. Many of us find it easier to carry a load of doubt or guilt or unresolved hostility than to let it out for resolution. Often it's a matter of childhood training or religious teaching. Whatever the causes or the reasons, these dammed-up conflicts often limit our self-fulfillment and the actualization of our potential for significant selfhood.

In the first article, Don Fabun, Director of Publications for Kaiser Aluminum and Chemical Corporation, attempts to explain one of the most pressing and visible areas of selves in conflict: the new youth.

In the second selection Rollo May, a psychologist, portrays for us a man who takes up residence in a cage. This story, a parable of sorts, should hold real meaning for those of us who "live in cages" in exchange for a token amount of security.

The Children of Change

Don Fabun

The young people we have called the new youth are described in penetrating and sympathetic detail by Don Fabun in his monograph, *The Children of Change*. Mr. Fabun is concerned that the series of connected and disconnected activities which collectively he calls The Movement might not be understood, and hence not taken seriously by the older generation.

He feels that by tying the current young generation in, historically and culturally, with The System, we who make up "The Establishment" can gain a clearer and more personal understanding of why The Movement has developed.

The Children of Change are the products of the collision, or at least the dissonance, between nineteenth-century rationalism, with its offspring twentieth-century technology, and institutions that were the products of the largely agrarian rural societies of the eighteenth and the seventeenth centuries. The technology changed; the institutions didn't, or at least very little.

The inputs of the rationalist-generated technology brought about, among others, these profound changes in technological societies:

From a predominantly agricultural society to a largely industrial one . . .

From a preponderantly rural and small town society to a largely urban and suburban one . . .

From an economy of scarcity, in which productivity was the primary goal, to an economy of abundance, in which consumption is the main goal and distribution the main problem . . .

From a geographically stable society to a highly mobile one . . .

From a relatively primitive communication system to a highly sophisticated one; informational time-lag gave way to instaneity . . .

From a labor-and-job oriented society to one increasingly aimed toward the use of leisure time . . .

From an emphasis on man-hour productivity to machine-investment productivity, with at least two concomitants; only the highly technically trained could participate in a meaningful and personally satisfying way of life in the economic system; many of the "small jobs" once available to the young or the poorly trained disappeared . . .

During all this time institutions remained very much the same.

The institutions continue to be run by a generation that finds it increasingly difficult to be in tune with the technological environment in which it finds itself. The Children of Change, on the other hand, have never experienced any other world but the technological one in which they are living.

For them two highly significant things happened: time collapsed and the horizon disappeared.

It was, more than anything else, TV that did it in this country. The child who is raised with the television tube experiences events instantaneously. He is constantly barraged by a succession of new products (which burst forth full-blown); new services (which would be his could he but afford them) and news of political and military events, some of which have not been "re-structured" by The Establishment. He wonders (if he is one of the Children of Change) why, then, it takes so long to get "anything done" in this society. His impatience with slow and "orderly" processes grows out of experience with the miraculous and the instantaneous.

Time collapsed—and the horizon disappeared. Unlike his forebears, whose horizon was the edge of the farm property, or end of a village street, the TV child saw events thousands of miles away as if they were only next door. In most cases he grew up knowing (by sight and sound) a presidential candidate better than the town mayor. Provincialism disappeared, his community became the world, and when this happened he had no real reason to respect local authority or that of his parents.

He walked out of a living room filled with miracles and found himself in a world where antiquated bureaucracies slowly pushed pieces of paper around. He knew what he wanted. He wanted miracles. And he wanted them *now*.

When a "child" in our post-industrial society leaves the protective womb of the TV tube to enter the world outside, it is like being reborn. He not only does not know *where* he is; he does not know *who* he is. Only now he is seventeen or eighteen with all the mental, emotional and physical abilities he is ever going to have. He is an adult in every respect but one—the law says he isn't.

(The magic age of twenty-one came from the Middle Ages. In that relatively low-protein society, it was twenty-one years before a male was strong enough to don armor and wield a sword, and thus become adult. Weirdly enough, this became for most of our society the age of "adulthood" and the right to vote.)

A voice from the back of the room suggests that the reason he isn't considered an adult is that he hasn't lived long enough. One replies, long enough for what? That age and wisdom are somehow related is not a concept that has been validated, scientifically or otherwise. And if "experience" is the criterion, then this "child" has probably accumuated more experience from the mass-media electronic society in his eighteen years than his parents have in their lifetimes.

So, a stranger in a strange land, he tries to find out where he is. And finds out he isn't where he thought he was. Remember his inputs. Conceptually most of them came from movies and television, some from comic books, a precious little from formal, conventional schooling, and perhaps a little from his family. Most of his knowledge of the "real" world he picked up in the streets, and mostly from other children in his own approximate age group.

For the most part (if he is going to become one of the Children of Change) he will have been raised in reasonable affluence. He probably has never suffered real hunger; stayed away from school because he did not have acceptable clothes, shoes, or transportation; never lacked for medical attention of a highly professional kind. He always had a recognizable identity, derived from a father whose profession was respected; lived at an "acceptable" address; and was furnished most, if not all, of the material things he wanted.

He probably never had to do any hard physical "work" in his life, unless it was to prepare himself physically for a sport; he probably never was in a situation where he couldn't place a collect telephone call home and get help. (Now, it is certainly a triumph of the industrialized society that, in one generation, it was possible to provide all this for him. But that is not the point. The point is that since he always has had these things, he takes them for granted. Just as most adults turn on the faucet and expect drinkable water to come out of it, without questioning.)

We have suggested that the style of The Movement, in this country, is essentially middle-class, non-ideological, Christian, and Western (as in a TV Western).

It is far too early in the game to give any more than a superficial accounting of what The Movement has accomplished—and what it has lost—so far. Nevertheless, an attempt will be made.

The gains:

American youth has established a place in our society that it did not enjoy before; it is a force to be reckoned with at every level.

The Movement has changed what was becoming an increasingly drab society into a riot of color and sound and light. If its own style was a kind of conformity, it was a new kind of conformity; at least everyone did not have to dress like pallbearers in order to sell a bar of soap. In some places, and at some times, our society began to take on the color and costumery of Mardi Gras, of the Renaissance, of Elizabethan England. A fresh wind blew through the forest; a few leaves jumped for joy.

On school campuses, some gains were made; not only for themselves, but for the generations to follow them. In many places, Victorian rules of conduct which applied only to them, and only on campus, were relaxed.

In some places, students were given at least a small voice in campus affairs; in the choice and relevancy of curricula, in freedom of speech and the right to participate in a society that is increasingly political.

The Movement has made genuine gains in directing attention to social and economic inequalities in our society and gave ethnic minority groups a sense of purpose and direction they did not have before. Some of these groups are now beginning to move under their own leadership to establish their own place in the social spectrum.

The Children of Change have made increasingly apparent the absurdity—and the tragedy—of substantial "pockets of poverty" in the midst of the most affluent society the world has ever known.

If they have been unable to stop the Vietnam War, they have caused the United States to examine its policies more closely, and to change some of them.

Again, through demonstrations and the subsequent publicity, they have caused a re-examination of the draft as it operates in a period of undeclared war.

They have caused the American people to re-examine a political system based on political nominating conventions and the process of the electoral college; both remnants of a day when politics had to be done from horseback. The Children of Change are rather aware that there are telephone, radio and television networks and that direct participation by every citizen in the political process is at least technologically possible.

Mostly because of television coverage of their own activities, they have made it clear that there is a significant difference between law enforcement and justice, and that perhaps a re-examination of "law and order" in this country is necessary. . . .

Most of all, the Children of Change have led many adult Americans to re-examine their way of life, their value system, and whether it any longer fits the world they live in. Despite its anti-intellectualism, The Movement is a little philosophic: it asks not "What?" or "How?" but "Why?"

For a revolution only thirteen years old, this is a rather impressive list of accomplishments. If The Movement should stop entirely tomorrow, it already has changed the style and mood of the American people. There is no reason to believe it will stop tomorrow.

There are many minuses, too.

As a result of the activities of the Children of Change, there has been a considerable damage to persons and property. In the U.S., in *thirteen years,* it appears to amount to 206 lives lost and about 162 millions in damage to property. This is little more than the loss of (152) lives in *one day* on U.S. highways and about equals the loss of property through highway accidents ($146 million) in five *days* on the highway.

Violence is the cutting edge of revolution. From the Boston Tea Party, through the Revolutionary War, the settling of the West, the Abolitionists, the trade union movement, the Volstead act, women's suffrage, it was violence that directed public attention to the social or economic problem that existed.

This is a violent country and its people are violent. This is not to say that others aren't—it is to say that we are. This country was taken at gun-point from its original inhabitants; and defended at gun-point. TV reinforces the concept that violence solves problems, twenty-four hours a day.

Much more important is that The Movement lacks a sense of the continuity of history; it does not seem to grasp (perhaps it has never been taught it; perhaps it wasn't listening) that our society, with whatever deficiencies it may have, has been built on the honest efforts of literally millions of people who may never have stood in a picket line or gone to jail, but who faced, and lived up to, the enormously more painful task of getting up every morning and going to work, to create the kind of affluence that makes *this* revolution possible.

The Movement lacks a sense of humor. It laughs at The Establishment, but does not seem capable of laughing at itself. It is as sternly Puritanistic and Calvinistic as The System it seeks to change. This may be its fatal flaw, for a movement that does not feel the essential absurdity of all human activity is blind in an essential way. When you can laugh at *yourself*—and not at others—the world holds no terrors for you.

But, basically, the greatest mistake of The Movement is that, by not controlling the cutting edge of its own violence, it has alienated many people who might otherwise have supported it.

It deserves better than that.

The Man Who Was Put in a Cage

Rollo May

Rather than try to explain anything about this article, we will simply let the author introduce it himself.

What a piece of work is man! how noble in reason! how infinite in faculty! in form and moving how express and admirable! . . . The paragon of animals!
                                                    —Shakespeare, *Hamlet*

From *Psychology and the Human Dilemma* by Rollo May, Copyright © 1967, by Litton Educational Publishing, Inc., by permission of Van Nostrand Reinhold Company.

We have quite a few discrete pieces of information these days about what happens to a person when he is deprived of this or that element of freedom. We have our studies of sensory deprivation and of how a person reacts when put in different kinds of authoritarian atmosphere, and so on. But recently I have been wondering what pattern would emerge if we put these various pieces of knowledge together. In short, what would happen to a living, whole person if his total freedom—or as nearly total as we can imagine—were taken away? In the course of these reflections, a parable took form in my mind.

The story begins with a king who, while standing in reverie at the window of his palace one evening, happened to notice a man in the town square below. He was apparently an average man, walking home at night, who had taken the same route five nights a week for many years. The king followed this man in his imagination—pictured him arriving home, perfunctorily kissing his wife, eating his late meal, inquiring whether everything was all right with the children, reading the paper, going to bed, perhaps engaging in the sex relation with his wife or perhaps not, sleeping, and getting up and going off to work again the next day.

And a sudden curiosity seized the king, which for a moment banished his fatigue: "I wonder what would happen if a man were kept in a cage, like the animals at the zoo?" His curiosity was perhaps in some ways not unlike that of the first surgeons who wondered what it would be like to perform a lobotomy on the human brain.

So the next day the king called in a psychologist, told him of his idea, and invited him to observe the experiment. When the psychologist demurred saying, "It's an unthinkable thing to keep a man in a cage," the monarch replied that many rulers had in effect, if not literally, done so, from the time of the Romans through Genghis Khan down to Hitler and the totalitarian leaders; so why not find out scientifically what would happen? Furthermore, added the king, he had made up his mind to do it whether the psychologist took part or not; he had already gotten the Greater Social Research Foundation to give a large sum of money for the experiment, and why let that money go to waste? By this time the psychologist also was feeling within himself a great curiosity about what would happen if a man were kept in a cage.

And so the next day the king caused a cage to be brought from the zoo—a large cage that had been occupied by a lion when it was new, then later by a tiger; just recently it had been the home of a hyena who died the previous week. The cage was put in an inner private court in the palace grounds, and the average man whom the king had seen from the window was brought and placed therein. The psychologist, with his Rorschach and Wechsler-Bellevue tests in his brief case to administer at some appropriate moment, sat down outside the cage.

At first the man was simply bewildered, and he kept saying to the psychologist, "I have to catch the tram, I have to get to work, look what time it is, I'll be late for work!" But later on in the afternoon the man began soberly to realize what was up, and then he protested vehemently, "The king can't do this to me! It is unjust! It's against the law." His voice was strong, and his eyes full of anger. The psychologist liked the man for his anger, and he became vaguely aware that this was a mood he had encountered often in people he worked with in his clinic. "Yes," he realized, "this anger is the attitude of people who—like the healthy adolescents of any era—want to fight what's wrong, who protest directly against it. When people come to the clinic in this mood, it is good—they can be helped."

During the rest of the week the man continued his vehement protests. When the king walked by the cage, as he did every day, the man made his protests directly to the monarch.

But the king answered, "Look here, you are getting plenty of food, you have a good bed, and you don't have to work. We take good care of you; so why are you objecting?"

After some days had passed, the man's protests lessened and then ceased. He was silent in his cage, generally refusing to talk. But the psychologist could see hatred glowing in his eyes. When he did exchange a few words, they were short, definite words uttered in the strong, vibrant, but calm voice of the person who hates and knows whom he hates.

Whenever the king walked into the courtyard, there was a deep fire in the man's eyes. The psychologist thought, "This must be the way people act when they are first conquered." He remembered that he had also seen that expression of the eyes and heard that tone of voice in many patients at his clinic: the adolescent who had been unjustly accused at home or in school and could do nothing about it; the college student who was required by public and campus opinion to be a star on the gridiron, but was required by his professors to pass courses he could not prepare for if he were to be successful in football—and who was then expelled from college for the cheating that resulted. And the psychologist, looking at the active hatred in the man's eyes, thought, "It is still good; a person who has this fight in him can be helped."

Every day the king, as he walked through the courtyard, kept reminding the man in the cage that he was given food and shelter and taken good care of, so why did he not like it? And the psychologist noticed that, whereas at first the man had been entirely impervious to the king's statements, it now seemed more and more that he was pausing for a moment after the king's speech—for a second the hatred was postponed from returning to his eyes—as though he were asking himself if what the king said were possibly true.

And after a few weeks more, the man began to discuss with the psychologist how it was a useful thing that a man is given food and shelter; and how man had to live by his fate in any case, and the part of wisdom was to accept fate. He soon was developing an extensive theory about security and the acceptance of fate, which sounded to the psychologist very much like the philosophical theories that Rosenberg and others worked out for the fascists in Germany. He was very voluble during this period, talking at length, although the talk was mostly a monologue. The psychologist noticed that his voice was flat and hollow as he talked, like the voice of people in TV previews who make an effort to look you in the eye and try hard to sound sincere as they tell you that you should see the program they are advertising, or the announcers on the radio who are paid to persuade you that you should like highbrow music.

And the psychologist also noticed that now the corners of the man's mouth always turned down, as though he were in some gigantic pout. Then the psychologist suddenly remembered: this was like the middle-aged, middle-class people who came to his clinic, the respectable bourgeois people who went to church and lived morally but who were always full of resentment, as though everything they did was conceived, born, and nursed in resentment. It reminded the psychologist of Nietzsche's saying that the middle class was consumed with resentment. He then for the first time began to be seriously worried about the man in the cage, for he knew that once resentment gets a firm start and becomes well rationalized and structuralized, it may become like cancer. When the person no longer knows whom he hates, he is much harder to help.

During this period the Greater Social Research Foundation had a board of trustees meeting, and they decided that since they were expending a fund to keep a man supported in a cage, it would look better if representatives of the Foundation at least visited the experiment. So a group of people, consisting of two professors and a few graduate students, came in one day to look at the man in the cage. One of the professors then proceeded to lecture to the group about the relation of the autonomic nervous system and the secretions of the ductless glands to human existence in a cage. But it occurred to the other professor that the verbal communications of the victim himself might just possibly be interesting, so he asked the man how he felt about living in a cage. The man was friendly toward the professors and students and explained to them that he had chosen this way of life, that there were great values in security and in being taken care of, that they would of course see how sensible his course was, and so on.

"How strange!" thought the psychologist, "and how pathetic; why is it he struggles so hard to get them to approve his way of life?"

In the succeding days when the king walked through the courtyard, the man fawned upon him from behind the bars in his cage and thanked him for the food and shelter. But when the king was not in the yard and the man was not aware that the psychologist was present, his expression was quite different—sullen and morose. When his food was handed to him through the bars by the keeper, the man would often drop the dishes or dump over the water and then would be embarrassed because of his stupidity and clumsiness. His conversation became increasingly one-tracked; and instead of the involved philosophical theories about the value of being taken care of, he had gotten down to simple sentences such as "It is fate," which he would say over and over again, or he would just mumble to himself, "It is." The psychologist was surprised to find that the man should now be so clumsy as to drop his food, or so stupid as to talk in those barren sentences, for he knew from his tests that the man had originally been of good average intelligence. Then it dawned upon the psychologist that this was the kind of behavior he had observed in some anthropological studies among the Negroes in the South—people who had been forced to kiss the hand that fed and enslaved them, who could no longer either hate or rebel. The man in the cage took more and more to simply sitting all day long in the sun as it came through the bars, his only movement being to shift his position from time to time from morning through the afternoon.

It was hard to say just when the last phase set in. But the psychologist became aware that the man's face now seemed to have no particular expression; his smile was no longer fawning, but simply empty and meaningless, like the grimace a baby makes when there is gas on its stomach. The man ate his food and exchanged a few sentences with the psychologist from time to time; but his eyes were distant and vague, and though he looked at the psychologist, it seemed that he never really *saw* him.

And now the man, in his desultory conversations, never used the word "I" any more. He had accepted the cage. He had no anger, no hate, no rationalizations. But he was now insane.

The night the psychologist realized this, he sat in his apartment trying to write a concluding report. But it was very difficult for him to summon up words, for he felt within himself a great emptiness. He kept trying to reassure himself with the words, "They say that nothing is ever lost, that matter is merely changed to energy and back again." But he could not help feeling that something *had* been lost, that something had gone out of the universe in this experiment.

He finally went to bed with his report unfinished. But he could not sleep; there was a gnawing within him which, in less rational and scientific ages, would have been called a conscience. Why didn't I tell the king that this is the one experiment that no man can do—or at least why didn't I shout that I would have nothing to do with the whole bloody business? Of course, the king would have dismissed me, the foundations would never have granted me any more money, and at the clinic they would have said that I was not a real scientist. But maybe one could farm in the mountains and make a living, and maybe one could paint or write something that would make future men happier and more free. . . .

But he realized that these musings were, at least at the moment, unrealistic, and he tried to pull himself back to reality. All he could get, however, was this feeling of emptiness within himself, and the words, "Something has been taken out of the universe, and there is left only a void."

Finally he dropped off to sleep. Some time later, in the small hours of the morning, he was awakened by a startling dream. A crowd of people had gathered, in the dream, in front of the cage in the courtyard, and the man in the cage—no longer inert and vacuous—was shouting through the bars of the cage in impassioned oratory. "It is not only I whose freedom is taken away!" he was crying. "When the king puts me or any man in a cage, the freedom of each one of you is taken away also. The king must go!" The people began to chant, "The king must go!" and they seized and broke out the iron bars of the cage, and wielded them for weapons as they charged the palace.

The psychologist awoke, filled by the dream with a great feeling of hope and joy—an experience of hope and joy probably not unlike that experienced by the free men of England when they forced King John to sign the Magna Charta. But not for nothing had the psychologist had an orthodox analysis in the course of his training, and as he lay surrounded by this aura of happiness, a voice spoke within him: "Aha, you had this dream to make yourself feel better; it's just a wish fulfillment."

"The hell it is!" said the psychologist as he climbed out of bed. "Maybe some dreams are to be acted on."

The
Authentic
Self

Throughout, our attempt has been to show ways in which each of us searches for the ways to experience his personal significance, his authenticity, his real selfhood. Those who live partial or conflicting lives, who never know they are really significant human beings, often require the intervention of another person.

Often this intervention is done by an act or word of love from a friend. Even total strangers have "worked wonders" in freeing a person's hidden potentials. Traditionally, people with incomplete or troubled lives have sought professional help, from their clergymen or from professionally-trained psychotherapists. Psychiatrists, psychologists, psychoanalysts, clinical social workers: all function in this capacity, though no two operate alike.

Psychotherapy is not a technique that promises a cure for a disease or conflict. It is a process-relationship—an involvement that is flexible, dynamic, changing, growing—that tries to reduce the conflicts and bring out the elements of full-functioning and actualization that have been blocked or lost in the person needing help.

In this section, April O'Connell and Terry O'Banion, from their book *The Shared Journey:*

An Introduction to Encounter, write about another experiment very popular today, the Encounter Group.

Hannah Green deftly and warmly describes the relationship between the girl, Deborah, and the psychiatrist, Dr. Fried, a warm and accepting woman. This is a fine illustration of the traditional therapeutic or "uncovering" process.

Self-Revealment as a Step Toward Encountering

Terry O'Banion and April O'Connell

One of the characteristics of "uptight," conflict-ridden, fearful, and insignificant-feeling people is their inability to disclose themselves to others. They usually lack self-awareness, too. One of the prime goals of the new forms of group experience is to help each person to "open up," to uncover some things about himself that enable others to know and appreciate him more. It is usually conceded that we often hide these things because we aren't sure how they will be received, or because they frighten, embarrass, or threaten us. The authors, two sensitive and insightful therapists, share their findings in this excerpt.

Some of you can probably discuss yourselves quite freely already; some may even have been doing this for most of your "verbal" life. Others, however, may recoil from exposing any aspect of yourselves which you feel is too private to share with another. Yet the ability to reveal ourselves, the ability to say, "This is who I am, this is what I am like, this is what concerns me, these are my beliefs," is one aspect of the ability to achieve human encounter.

For the sake of those who may be hesitant to discuss their deepest feelings, let us take a moment to explore some of the reasons for the need to be "on our guard" with other people.

Many of us have been brought up to believe that "wearing one's

heart on one's sleeve," showing "weakness" or "one's feelings," is something to be ashamed of, something somehow a little improper—something to be avoided, in other words. In some groups, for example, to
show strong emotional feelings is regarded as perhaps even a bit un-
civilized. Showing of emotion in public may appear almost as unseemly
as the display of other bodily functions.

Some of us have been taught that revealing our true feelings (what
we really are, here and now) has no place in a "polite" society; that the
considerate person, even in the midst of emotional crises, "keeps things
to himself," or "puts on a good front," or "acts as if nothing is the matter." In fact, some societies—particularly the pre-Westernized cultures
of the East—followed this behavior pattern to such lengths that Orientals
were epitomized as "inscrutable." Actually, the cultured Chinese or
Japanese had developed the astonishing skill of smiling under extreme
duress (anger, fear, sadness, terror); and on the opposite side of the coin,
of maintaining a high degree of solemnity when most elated. Part of this
behavior may be attributed to "saving face" or regarded as a protective
device against the anger of jealous men or gods; but another aspect of
Oriental behavior stemmed from respect for the feeling of others around
them. Orientals believed (as many of us do) that it is not considerate
either to display pride and conceit over one's good fortune, or to burden
others with one's misfortunes.

Those of us who have been brought up in an Anglo-Saxon tradition
have been strongly influenced by this same kind of attitude. The English
language abounds in expressions for the necessity or the propriety of not
exposing our real feelings or inner thoughts. We "guard our tongues,"
or "keep a stiff upper lip." Small boys are admonished daily to "act like
a man," which usually means not to cry in public.

Your authors admire as much as anyone those people who do not
waste words, who cannot be accused of "chattering," who "do more
than they say," who use their words wisely. We both have a background
in English and both have a reverence for the careful use of our language. In no way do we wish to encourage indiscriminate babbling. But
although there may be a time and a place to be silent, in the process of
self-revealment "guarding one's tongue" can hinder the process of communication with others. It is difficult to get to know someone who main-
tains a constant reserve, who does not open up to you as a person, or
who "plays it cool." We can admire the character of such a person but

it may be difficult to feel warmth with and toward him. It is written in Ecclesiastes that there is "a time to be silent and a time to speak." The process of encountering is surely "a time to speak."

While some of us have been steeped in the attitude of keeping a reserve about ourselves since childhood, others of us may have adopted it out of fear of being hurt, or rejected, or ridiculed. When asked to express their feelings of anxiety about revealing themselves to others, students have said:

> "I am afraid I'll be laughed at. I was always a fat girl and people never took me seriously."
>
> "I'm afraid if I really open up to someone, and show them what I am really like, they'll be shocked."
>
> "I don't trust people. When people get to know a lot about you, they have power over you."
>
> "I've been hurt by people I thought were my friends. I don't intend to get hurt any more."

In a beginning encountering group, therefore, it is necessary to share anxieties and fears that the participants may have about self-revealment. Sometimes by merely bringing these anxieties out in the open the person finds the imaginary indictments of others are groundless and the ghosts of previous hurts are laid to rest.

Another facet of human encounter groups that must be discussed is *the principle of confidentiality*. Each member makes a pledge that what goes on in the group remains there—is not talked about to outsiders. It is a sacred trust. Any encounter group must begin with the primary rule that what goes on in the group, what is said by members of that group, is held to be as sacred as the confessional or the revelations of client to lawyer. For there is nothing of the quality of being on trial in an encounter group, nor of having to confess things to others. Each one has a right at all times to maintain privacy—there is no obligation to reveal anything. Indeed, it is difficult to imagine anyone being able to coerce such things out of group members. Nevertheless, it does become easier for people to become self-revealing, in spite of anxiety, when the participants of the group have committed themselves to confidentiality. By the way, this pledging of confidentiality seems necessary in encounter groups only at the beginning of the meetings; as the group continues to meet, an attitude of mutual trust and responsibility to that trust seems to develop quite naturally. The people in the group come to take the attitude of confidentiality quite as a matter of course, as if there had never been any other attitude to begin with.

We can now turn our attention to the outcomes of self-revealment. First, there is the obvious therapeutic release which comes of being able to speak of some of the things we have been afraid to discuss with others. Sometimes, merely getting these worries out in the open is enough to dissolve them (just the sympathetic listening of someone else is enough to lighten a burden). For example, one young man wrote:

> I have realized that people have taken time to talk about my problem. Two people especially have given their time to me. These two helped me to understand myself and others. For years I have been looking for something, but did not realize what it was. They helped me as I found a place and purpose in our meetings.

Another group member, remarking on the growing bond between the members of this group, wrote:

> We feel that the other person is at least listening (whether he agrees or not) and we will listen to him. So we are discussing, not arguing, with each other.

But at a "deeper" level, self-revealment does someting more than provide therapeutic release. In 1956, a writer named Colin Wilson published a book called *The Outsider,* in which he attempted to characterize the present age as one of existential meaninglessness; he wrote that the reaction to this meaninglessness resulted in a "sick" society, and that the symptoms are revealed in our era as boredom, alienation, and the inability to "lay hold of experience." Although his theme was not new,* Wilson did focus, by way of his title, on the loneliness modern man feels —that he is perhaps looking at life and other men, but is not involved *with* them. He experiences himself as separate, and phenomenologically speaking, as an outsider.

We are not prepared to debate the existential meaning or meaninglessness of life at this moment. Our own reaction is rather personal: When we are involved with and committed to mankind, even in that small aspect of it that we touch as wife, husband, mother, father, teacher,

---

*Among some of the writers who have been concerned with man's alienation are: Fromm, Sartre, Camus, Samuel Beckett, Ionesco, Heidegger . . . the list is long.

and friend, we find meaning. When *I* and *Thou* (to use Buber's phrase) reveal ourselves to each other and recognize each other as inhabitants of the same phenomenological world, I and Thou are inside the circle of human relation.

To the extent, then, that we can open ourselves to another human being, to that extent do we feel ourselves as part of the society of men— related to them and they to us. We are no longer *outside*, but *within* a circle of human belongingness.

As we reveal ourselves, as we permit others to reveal themselves, we are able to take off the masks, the armor, that we use to keep people from knowing us. Eliot said succinctly that we "put on a face to meet the faces that we meet." For as we become less hidden, and more open with each other, we realize that *we are capable of reaching toward each other* across our physical separateness. And, ultimately, there occurs the phenomenon, the diamond-like moment of emotional and spiritual communion, of human encountering. Let us quote, though, from the writings of the students who have experienced this quality of belonging—this feeling of being an *insider*.

> I feel great at times and at other times I have a feeling I can't explain as yet but it is one I am aware of, I know is there but I don't know what to do with it yet. Somehow, I don't feel alone anymore. I feel that I am a part of people.
>
> I feel much freer, a feeling of not being so alone since we started this term. I feel now there is some hope, a hope for the future which was lacking at the beginning of the term. I feel a comradeship for the first time in my life with one or two other people in this class and that helps immensely. . . .
>
> I guess the purpose of this course is to encounter other people. . . . This course gives you the wonderful feeling of being wanted and also that there are people who care about you and this is very important in life, what keeps you going. To feel not wanted, out of place, or left out is terrible, is miserable.

If we have helped students to feel related to others around them, if we have done nothing more than help them to feel like insiders, then this kind of a course has been justified. We believe that helping people to achieve human encounter should be one of the main concerns of educational institutions, and, for that matter, of all institutions.

Up to now, we have spoken of two outcomes of self-revealment: the therapeutic release of one's inner concerns and the experience of involvement and belonging. A third outcome of self-revealment entails the affirmation of oneself while in communication (that is to say, in communion with others). As we give voice to that which we are, to that which is central to our being, we *affirm ourselves;* even as we become involved in the community of man, our existence as separate and unique entities is clarified and affirmed. This affirmation is something more than merely not conforming to some outside societal pressure; it is something deeper than a mere inflated ego; it is something more positive than the confirmation of your existence or your right to be. It is the exciting discovery of *your* awareness of *your* uniqueness from all others at the deepest level of your being. This third outcome was the one most frequently alluded to by the members of one class committed to the goal of human encountering. Here are some of the various ways they expressed it:

> In the sharing of experiences in this class, the student has the opportunity of evaluating himself and his needs. By encountering the other members of the class, whether meaningfully or superficially, he enlarges himself and begins to look within himself.

> In this course, the student should learn about others and through transposition, himself. I know I have. It is through others that one sees himself. The class members should feel free to reveal themselves when they feel it is the time.

> . . . I somehow started thinking deeper about things, to care more about myself and other people.

> This class has given me a chance to stop and try to see who I am and where I am going.

> This course is for the enlarging of the minds of everyone who is introduced to, or given the chance to participate in, this type of class. . . .

> Participation will advance as the students' minds and hearts open up and advance.

> I am a better person because of this course for now I think more deeply about such topics as love, death, and life.

> The purpose of this study is to "open the door" to the student, to open his mind, his heart, and his mouth. By seeing himself, something in common with others, and differences in others, he may encounter himself and recognize others as persons, not people.

from *I Never Promised You a Rose Garden*

Hannah Green

Deborah Blau is sixteen. She is also a girl who lives in two worlds, ours and her own special world, the Kingdom of Yr. She has been diagnosed schizophrenic. In her need to escape from reality's tortures, she fantasizes a Kingdom in which she is at first a princess. In the Kingdom of Yr, there are gods and demons and people like The Collect. In the process of treatment, she gradually allows her therapist, Dr. Fried, to know about the Kingdom of Yr. The doctor's name in Yri is Furii, meaning "Fire-Touch." As Dr. Fried becomes closer to Deborah, the girl finds the creatures of Yr gradually turning on her, punishing her for her "betrayal."

Dr. Fried hasn't promised that life in the "real world" would be any kind of easy thing, "a rose garden," but she has promised to be with her, to help her learn how to face the rough parts.

In this excerpt we find Deborah experiencing the early conflicts of giving up life in Yr and taking a fuller part in the world of reality.

For Deborah, the backfires became the only way of easing the pressure of the stifled volcano inside her. She continued to burn the same places over and over, setting layers of burns on top of one another. Cigarette butts and matches were easy to obtain, although they were supposedly guarded with great care; even D ward's precautions were no match for the intensity of her need. Because the effects of the burnings lasted only an hour or so and because she could only bear the building up of pressure for three or four hours, she had to have a large supply of used cigarettes and the matches to relight them.

For a few days the wounds remained secret, even though she had to change the site of the burning when they began to infect and drain. She was amused but not surprised at how oblivious the nurses and attendants were. The wounds drained and stank and no one noticed. She thought: It's because they don't really want to look at us.

At the end of the week, the new doctor came up to the ward again. "You look a lot better," he said, stopping by Deborah in the dayroom.

"I ought to," she said a little acidly, "I've had to work like hell to keep it up."

"Well, with such an improvement, you should be ready to go back to B ward very soon."

When she heard this, she realized that B ward, with its unprotected time and free matches, was a perfect chance for the death she thought she wanted. Then she noticed that she was terrified, and wondered why. If he was letting her die as she wished, why was she angry?

"I have some more burns," she said simply.

He looked shocked, recovered quickly, and said, "I'm glad you told me."

She began to pull on her sweater, twisting it like wet laundry in her hands. *If I want to die, what am I saving myself for?* she demanded, still angry at the mental image of him permitting her to burn herself to death on B ward.

You told him because you are a coward! the Collect said. They began the old jibes again.

"How is the old sore?" the doctor said, loosening the bandaged place. She did not answer him because he was seeing for himself. The burn was stubbornly refusing to heal. "You haven't done any more to this?" he asked, a little bit accusingly and afraid to make it stronger.

"No," she said.

"We'll try another kind of bandage. Let me see the new burn." He looked at the other arm. "How many times did you burn this?"

"About eight."

He bandaged both places and left, no doubt to scold the nurses about the carelessness of leaving dangerous, fire-making materials on the ward. The burning cigarette he left behind him in the dayroom was long enough for two series of burnings.

When the lawgivers of D ward discovered that its patients were not so safe as they had thought, they swept the ward up and down with reforms to widen still further the distance between themselves and the patients. The fork that had been introduced on "D" a year before was now rescinded. The Age of Metal gave way to the Age of Wood and fire prevailed only within the precincts of the nursing station, the modern era. In the pleistocene beyond, Pithecanthropus erectus shambled and muttered gibberish, ate with its fingers, and wet on the floor.

"Thanks a lot, kid," Lee Miller said sarcastically as she walked past Deborah into the lighted place where Modern Man supplied the patients with his status-symbols—cigarette and match.

"Go to Hell," Deborah answered, but her tone lacked conviction. Later, the Wife of the Abdicated accused her of being a spy and in league with the Secretary of the Interior, and as Deborah already knew, the Secretary of the Interior was one of the worst Enemies.

Getting matches and butts now became difficult, but by no means impossible. Modern Man was careless with the fire-tipped cylinders he burned and breathed, and waiting beside him was a fire-hungry primitive whose gray and flat world magically included the cigarette in sharp focus, color, smell, and three dimensions of form.

But firing back at the volcano did not change its surface, its granite garment, as Anterrabae called it. And gods and Collect and Censor were wildly and inexplicably free with the Punishment. Even the logic of Yr seemed to have been erased and the laws overturned. Deborah began to believe that the volcano would erupt and explode. She remembered that the Last Deception had not yet come.

The days had long since become an Earth-form that was only a grammatical nicety. She woke up in one of them and found herself in pack, as so often before. A key turned in the lock of the door and a nurse entered. Behind the nurse, looking unbelievably different because she had not changed at all, stood Furii.

"All right," she said, and came in. The nurse brought a chair for her, and Deborah began to wish that she might escape the woman's face and the disgust she saw in it. Furii looked all around, sat beside the bed, and nodded with a kind of awe.

"My goodness!"

"You're back," Deborah said. The self-hate, terror, shame, pity, vanity, and despair never crossed the stone surface. "Did you have a good time?"

"My goodness," Furii repeated. "What happened? You were doing very well when I left, and now, back here. . . ." She looked around again.

Deborah was afraid of the joy she felt in seeing Furii alive. She said, "You've seen this . . . awfulness before; why are you so shocked?"

"Yes, I have seen it. I am only sorry to see you in it, and suffering so much."

Deborah closed her eyes. She was stricken with shame and she wanted to escape to the Pit, to be dark and blank, but Furii was back and there was no hiding place. Her mind held. "I didn't know you were coming."

"It is the day I said I would be back," Furii said.

"It is?"

"It is, and I think maybe you got in this bad shape to tell me how angry you are that I went off and left you."

"That's not true—" Deborah said. "I tried with Royson—I really did, but you were dead—at least I thought you were—and he wanted only to prove how right he was and how smart. I forgot that you would come back. . . ."

She began to thrash again, even though she was exhausted. "I'm all stopped and closed . . . like it was before I came here . . . only the volcano is burning hotter and hotter while the surface doesn't even know if it is alive or not!"

The doctor moved closer. "It is one of these times," she said quietly, "when what you say is most important."

Deborah pushed her head hard into the bed. "I can't even sort them out—the words."

"Well then, just let it come to us."

"Are you that strong?"

"We are both that strong."

Deborah took a breath. "I am poisonous and I hate it. I am going to be destroyed in shame and degradation and I hate it. I hate myself and the deceivers. I hate my life and my death. For my truth the world gives only lies; I tried with Royson time after time, but I saw that all he wanted was to be right. He might as well have said, 'Come to your senses and stop the silliness'—what they said for the years and years when I was disappointing them on the surface and lying to them with the inmost part of Yr and me and the enemy soldier. God curse me! God curse me!"

A soft scraping sound, a breathed rasp, came after, as she tried to cry, but the sound of it was so ridiculous and ugly that she soon stopped.

"Maybe when I leave," Furii said, "you can learn to cry. For now, let me say this: measure the hate you feel now, and the shame. That quantity is your capacity also to love and to feel joy and to have compassion. Also, I will see you tomorrow."

She left.

That evening Miss Coral came to Deborah holding a book. "Look," she said timidly, "my doctor has left this with me. It is a book of plays and I wondered if perhaps you might not wish to read them with me."

Deborah looked over at Helene, who was sitting against the wall. Had Helene been offering the book, she would have kicked it across the floor to Deborah, perhaps with a taunt. Did any two people, even in the World, speak the same language?

As she answered, Deborah could hear herself mirroring some of Miss Coral's elaborate form of speech and also her shyness. "Which one would you prefer?" Miss Coral asked. They began to read *The Importance of Being Earnest,* with Deborah doing most of the men and Miss Coral doing most of the women. Soon Lee and Helene and Fiorentini's Mary were reading, too. With the actors parodying themselves, the play was uproarious. Mary, laugh and all, was Ernest as a well-born bedlamite, while Miss Coral as Sybil reeked with magnolias and spiderwebs. Oscar Wilde's urbane and elegant comedy was being presented on the nightmare canvas of Hieronymus Bosch. They read the whole play through, and then another, aware that the attendants were laughing with them as well as at them, and thinking, for all the fear it caused, that it was a good night; one which, magically, was not included in their damnation.

Esther Blau faced Doctor Fried unable to speak Then she cleared her throat.

"Did I understand you correctly?"

"I think so, but first——"

"Why! Why?"

"We are attempting to find out why."

"Can't you find out *before* she's burnt up!"

Esther had read the carefully general report, but something in its tone had alerted her and she had come down again, full of foreboding, to see Deborah. She had been told that it would be unwise; she had demanded to see Dr. Halle, and once in his office, she had heard the facts no word could modify or ease. Now she sat before Dr. Fried, angry and frightened and despairing.

"And what can I tell her father—what lie can I tell him now so that we can keep her here where she gets sicker and more violent all the time!"

Through her fear the doctor's words sounded long and slow. "I think perhaps that we are all letting ourselves go overboard with this burning business. It is, after all, a symptom of the sickness which we all know is there, and which is *still* responding to treatment."

"But it's so . . . *so ugly!*"

"You mean the wounds?"

"I haven't seen the wounds—I mean the idea, the thought. How could anyone do that to themselves! A person would be in——" Esther gasped and put her hand before her mouth, and tears spilled over the rims of her eyes and rolled down her face.

"No, no," the doctor said, "It's the *word* that is making you so frightened. It is the old evil word 'insane,' which once meant 'hopeless and forever,' that is making you suffer so."

"I never let myself think that word for Debby!"

The façade is broken and what is behind the façade is not so bad, Dr. Fried thought. She wondered if she could let the mother know it in some way. It might be a small comfort. The telephone rang and Dr. Fried answered it in her affable voice, and when she turned again to face Esther, she found her composed.

"You do think, then, that there is still a chance for her to be . . . normal?"

"I think that there is certainly a chance for her to be mentally healthy and strong. I will say something to you now, Mrs. Blau, but it is not for your daughter and I will appreciate it if you never mention it to her. I am approached at least four times every week to do therapy with a patient. I have doctor's analyses also to supervise for the university School of Psychiatry, and at every session I must turn many away. I would be worse than wasteful to give a moment's time to a hopeless case. I do not keep her one moment longer than I think I can help her. Tell them this at home. You need not keep telling lies—the truth is not unbearable at all."

The doctor saw Deborah's mother out of her office, hoping that she had helped. Easy comfort might do for some other branch of medicine (placebo was a prescription more common than doctors themselves liked to admit), but the whole weight of her life and training was against it. And after her experiences, anything that sounded even faintly like placating would frighten Esther Blau; if she had been strengthened by this talk, the whole family would be strengthened in turn.

Dr. Fried understood that Esther had outgrown her subjection to her father. She was now a strong, dominant, even dominating person. The same force in her that had tried to conquer all of Deborah's enemies, to her detriment, might be the saving force as well. If she believed in this therapy for her daughter, she would stand against the whole family to see that it was carried out. Deborah's illness had done more than shake the portraits in the family album. Some of the family had had to question why, and had grown a little themselves because of asking. If this were true, it was a source of hope seldom mentioned in the psychiatric journals, maybe because it was beyond "science" and beyond planning for. Outside the doors of study, Dr. Fried's father had once told her, an angel waits.

Coming out of the doctor's house into the brisk autumn day, Esther looked toward the high, heavily screened porch behind which she knew was D ward. What was it like there? What was it like inside the minds of people who had to stay there? She looked away from it quickly, finding that it was blurred by a sudden overwhelming of tears.

Deborah sat on the floor of the ward having her burns dressed. She had begun to be of medical interest; the wounds refused to heal. The student nurses, delighted by so tangible a condition, worked faithfully and busily with their unguents, potions, bandages, and tape. The smokers were still angry at Deborah, holding her responsible for the new rules, and even Lee, who needed to talk, was sending scornful looks at her. While the nurses worked, Deborah watched what she had come to call the Breathing Frieze of other patients, sitting and standing, expressionless except for a look of great awe that their blood could move its ways so steadily, their hearts could beat beyond will or passion. When the nurses finished dressing the recalcitrant burns, they left the hall for a moment. Out of the corner of her eye, Deborah became aware that Helene was looking hard at Sylvia, who was standing next to her, immobile as ever. The next moment, Helene came close and struck Sylvia heavily once, and once again. Sylvia stood beneath the blows and gave no sign of being conscious of them. Challenged, Helene exploded into a whirlwind of rage. A wild creature seemed to be hurling itself against rock. Helene beat and screamed and scratched and flapped, spitting and redfaced, her hair flying. Sylvia reacted only by closing her eyes slowly. Her hands were still limp at her sides; her body, it seemed, was totally commended to the forces of gravity and inertia; she appeared to take no interest in the beating. The sudden, swift happening was interrupted by the standard six attendants required to get Helene away. Soon she was borne off drowning in a wave of khaki and white.

Deborah remained standing ten feet from Sylvia. Both of them seemed alone on the planet. Deborah remembered the time two years earlier when Helene had rushed at her to destroy the face that had witnessed, and be safe from its knowledge. Everything had been Helene—doctors, nurses, attendants, the ward's quickened rhythm, the wet sheets, and seclusion—all, all Helene, and Deborah had stood alone and shamed, because she had been too degraded to defend herself. She had stood as Sylvia was standing now, like a statue. Only her breathing betrayed her, wrenching in and out, almost as if she were snorting. Deborah was the only one who could know why Sylvia, who had failed to defend herself, needed as much attention as Helene was now getting.

I should go to her and touch her on the shoulder and say something, Deborah thought. But she stood still. I should go because it happened to me and no one knows as I do, how it is. . . . But her feet were in her shoes and her shoes were not moving toward Sylvia, and her hands stayed at her sides and were not moving. In the name of the dark night together when she broke her silence for me, I should go. . . . And she tried to wrench free of her granite garments and stone shoes. She looked at Sylvia, the ugliest of all of the patients, with her drooling and her pale, waxy face in its frozen grimace, and she knew that if she went to give what she of all people knew was needed, Sylvia might destroy her with silence alone. A fear came up to consume the wish to act. In another moment the subduers of Helene began to come back from the battle and the chance was lost. From the subsiding fear, shame rose. It grew up over her face so that she stood for a long time stone blind and wishing for death.

Later, she stood before Furii in the office and told her what she had seen and had not done.

"I never told you a lie!" Deborah said. "I never told you that I was human. Now you can throw me out because I have a guilt with no apology."

"I am not here to excuse you," Furii said, looking up at Deborah from the chair, and lighting a cigarette. "You will find no shortage of moral issues and hard decisions in the real world, and, as I have said before, it's no rose garden. Let us bless the strength that let you see, and work toward the time when you will be able also to *do* what you see to do. We have now to work hard on the roots of this burning which you do in your anger at me and at the hospital."

Almost at once Deborah knew that Furii was wrong about the reason for the burning and the need for it, and most wrong about its seriousness. While it had the semblance of terrible aberration, Deborah felt that this was as deceptive as the quiet slopes of her volcano.

"Do you think the burning is very serious?" she asked Furii.

"Most serious, indeed," Furii answered.

"You are wrong," Deborah said simply, hoping that the doctor really believed what she had so often said about the patient trusting her own deep beliefs. There were over forty burns, inflicted over and over again on flesh scraped raw to receive them, and yet they didn't seem worth the fuss that was being made about them.

"I don't know why, but you are wrong."

Deborah looked around the cluttered office. For members of he world, sunlight was streaming through the windows, but its goldenness and warmth were only there for her to perceive from a distance. The air around her was still cold and dark. It was this eternal estrangement, not fire against her flesh, that was the agony.

"Restricted or not," she murmured, "I will do penance."

"Louder, please, I cannot hear you."

"Selective inattention," Deborah said, laughing at the words of psychiatry, whose private language and secret jargon had not the beauty or poetry of Yri. Furii saw, too, and laughed.

"Sometimes I think that our professional vocabulary goes too far, but we speak to one another after all, and not only to ourselves and the falling gods. Was it to them that you spoke just now?"

"No," Deborah said, "to you. I have decided not to be immoral, because of what happened to Sylvia. If I couldn't do what I should have done after Helene attacked her, at least I won't implicate her in my burnings, since you say that they are serious."

"How do you mean this?"

"She smokes sometimes, but she is forgetful. She has put cigarettes down when I was there to pick them up quickly and be gone. Both Marys smoke like wild women and all I have to do is make sure that no one spots me. They are contributing to my delinquency, aren't they?"

"I suppose, in a way they are. Actually you are taking advantage of their symptoms."

"That must not be allowed to happen," Deborah said quietly. She wondered why Furii had left matches in her waiting room, and cigarettes, too. The nurse who had accompanied her was easily distracted; Deborah wondered if Furii knew how trying those minutes of waiting had been.

When the time was over, Deborah got up to leave, saying, "I am cutting my throat now myself. I won't steal burning butts from the patients unless they're left in the ash trays or are forgotten, and I won't let you contribute either because you wouldn't want to."

Then she reached into her sleeve and drew out the two packs of matches she had taken from Furii's table and threw them angrily on the paper-littered desk.

The Transcending Self

Man is one in his nature, but often experiences himself in other ways. All men everywhere have found it necessary to relate themselves to something outside or other than themselves. Man does many things in his attempt to "get outside" his ordinary flesh-locked existence. He utilizes religion and a variety of "cultic" behaviors to experience something "more."

Man has always been interested in the mystical, the odd, the exotic, the other-worldly. In his interest, partly from curiosity, and partly because he hoped to relate himself to something Other, he has done many interesting and also desperate things.

Psychiatrist Ronald Laing discusses the transcendent experience in the excerpt from his book, *The Politics of Experience*. He makes a strong case for the necessity of getting out of one's self and relating to a larger reality.

Alan Watts is a many-faceted man: Zen devotee, Taoist, Anglican priest, lay psychologist, and writer. He is an advocate of the larger reality, feeling that man has a "metaphysical instinct." He has recently come out in favor of LSD and other mind-expanding drugs as shortcuts to transcendence.

Transcendental Experience

Ronald Laing

Man is insecure because he is limited in his knowledge of many things; about none of these things is he as ignorant as he is about himself.

How do we find ourselves? We do it in the way advocated by mystics of old, by "losing ourselves." Laing believes that the experience of psychosis may be a necessary one for some people. Others may have to experiment with transcending behavior, which includes drugs, alcohol, music, and other types of "skinless" behavior. We present his views for their value in provoking your thinking, not as final answers to this enormous problem.

We are living in an age in which the ground is shifting and the foundations are shaking. I cannot answer for other times and places. Perhaps it has always been so. We know it is true today.

In these circumstances, we have every reason to be insecure. When the ultimate basis of our world is in question, we run to different holes in the ground, we scurry into roles, statuses, identities, interpersonal relations. We attempt to live in castles that can only be in the air because there is no firm ground in the social cosmos on which to build. We are all witnesses to this state of affairs. Each sometimes sees the same fragment of the whole situation differently; often our concern is with different presentations of the original catastrophe.

In this chapter I wish to relate the transcendental experiences that *sometimes* break through in psychosis, to those experiences of the divine that are the living fount of all religion. . . .

Experience may be judged as invalidly mad or as validly mystical. The distinction is not easy. In either case, from a social point of view, such judgments characterize different forms of behavior, regarded in our society as deviant. People behave in such ways because their experi-

From *The Politics of Experience* by Ronald D. Laing, pp. 131–145. Reprinted by permission of Penguin Books Ltd.

ence of themselves is different. It is on the existential meaning of such unusual experience that I wish to focus.

Psychotic experience goes beyond the horizons of our common, that is, our communal, sense.

What regions of experience does this lead to? It entails a loss of the usual foundations of the "sense" of the world that we share with one another. Old purposes no longer seem viable; old meanings are senseless; the distinctions between imagination, dream, external perceptions often seem no longer to apply in the old way. External events may seem magically conjured up. Dreams may seem to be direct communications from others; imagination may seem to be objective reality.

But most radical of all, the very ontological foundations are shaken. The being of phenomena shifts and the phenomenon of being may no longer present itself to us as before. There are no supports, nothing to cling to, except perhaps some fragments from the wreck, a few memories, names, sounds, one or two objects, that retain a link with a world long lost. This void may not be empty. It may be peopled by visions and voices, ghosts, strange shapes and apparitions. No one who has not experienced how insubstantial the pageant of external reality can be, how it may fade, can fully realize the sublime and grotesque presences that can replace it, or that can exist alongside it.

When a person goes mad, a profound transposition of his place in relation to all domains of being occurs. His center of experience moves from ego to self. Mundane time becomes merely anecdotal, only the eternal matters. The madman is, however, confused. He muddles ego with self, inner with outer, natural and supernatural. Nevertheless, he can often be to us, even through his profound wretchedness and disintegration, the heirophant of the sacred. An exile from the scene of being as we know it, he is an alien, a stranger signaling to us from the void in which he is foundering, a void which may be peopled by presences that we do not even dream of. They used to be called demons and spirits, and they used to be known and named. He has lost his sense of self, his feelings, his place in the world as we know it. He tells us he is dead. But we are distracted from our cosy security by this mad ghost who haunts us with his visions and voices which seem so senseless and of which we feel impelled to rid him, cleanse him, cure him.

Madness need not be all breakdown. It may also be breakthrough. It is potentially liberation and renewal as well as enslavement and existential death.

There are now a growing number of accounts by people who have been through the experience of madness.*

The following is part of one of the earlier contemporary accounts, as recorded by Karl Jaspers in his *General Psychopathology.*†

I believe I caused the illness myself. In my attempt to penetrate the other world I met its natural guardians, the embodiment of my own weaknesses and faults. I first thought these demons were lowly inhabitants of the other world who could play me like a ball because I went into these regions unprepared and lost my way. Later I thought they were split-off parts of my own mind (passions) which existed near me in free space and thrived on my feelings. I believed everyone else had these too but did not perceive them, thanks to the protective successful deceit of the feeling of personal existence. I thought the latter was an artifact of memory, thought-complexes, etc., a doll that was nice enough to look at from outside but nothing real inside it.

In my case the personal self had grown porous because of my dimmed consciousness. Through it I wanted to bring myself closer to the higher sources of life. I should have prepared myself for this over a long period by invoking in me a higher, impersonal self, since "nectar" is not for mortal lips. It acted destructively on the animal-human self, split it up into its parts. These gradually disintegrated, the doll was really broken and the body damaged. I had forced untimely access to the "source of life," the curse of the "gods" descended on me. I recognized too late that murky elements had taken a hand. I got to know them after they had already too much power. There was no way back. I now had the world of spirits I had wanted to see. The demons came up from the abyss, as guardian Cerberi, denying admission to the unauthorized. I decided to take up the life-and-death struggle. This meant for me in the end a decision to die, since I had to put aside everything that maintained the enemy, but this was also everything that maintained life. I wanted to enter death without going mad and stood before the Sphinx: either thou into the abyss or I!

Then came illumination. I fasted and so penetrated into the true nature of my seducers. They were pimps and deceivers of my dear personal self which seemed as much a thing of naught as they. A larger and more comprehensive self emerged and I could abandon

---

*See, for example, the anthology *The Inner World of Mental Illness,* edited by Bert Kaplan (New York and London: Harper and Row, 1964), and *Beyond All Reason,* by Morag Coate (London: Constable and Co., 1964; Philadelphia: Lippincott, 1965).

†Manchester: Manchester University Press, 1962, pages 417–18.

the previous personality with its entire entourage. I saw this earlier personality could never enter transcendental realms. I felt as a result a terrible pain, like an annihilating blow, but I was rescued, the demons shriveled, vanished and perished. A new life began for me and from now on I felt different from other people. A self that consisted of conventional lies, shams, self-deceptions, memory images, a self just like that of other people, grew in me again but behind and above it stood a greater and more comprehensive self which impressed me with something of what is eternal, unchanging, immortal and inviolable and which ever since that time has been my protector and refuge. I believe it would be good for many if they were acquainted with such a higher self and that there are people who have attained this goal in fact by kinder means.

Jaspers comments:

Such self-interpretations are obviously made under the influence of delusion-like tendencies and deep psychic forces. They originate from profound experiences and the wealth of such schizophrenic experience calls on the observer as well as on the reflective patient not to take all this merely as a chaotic jumble of contents. Mind and spirit are present in the morbid psychic life as well as in the healthy. But interpretations of this sort must be divested of any casual importance. All they can do is to throw light on content and bring it into some sort of context.

This patient has described, with a lucidity I could not improve upon, a very ancient quest, with its pitfalls and dangers. Jaspers still speaks of this experience as morbid and tends to discount the patient's own construction. Yet both the experience and the construction may be valid in their own terms.

Certain *transcendental experiences* seem to me to be the original wellspring of all religions. Some psychotic people have transcendental experiences. Often (to the best of their recollection), they have never had such experiences before, and frequently they will never have them again. I am not saying, however, that psychotic experience necessarily contains this element more manifestly than sane experience.

We experience in different modes. We perceive external realities, we dream, imagine, have semiconscious reveries. Some people have visions, hallucinations, experience faces transfigured, see auras and so on. Most people most of the time experience themselves and others in one or another way that I shall call *egoic*. That is, centrally or peripherally, they experience the world and themselves in terms of a consistent identity, a me-here over against a you-there, within a framework of certain ground structures of space and time shared with other members of their society.

This identity-anchored, space-and-time-bound experience has been studied philosophically by Kant, and later by the phenomenologists, e.g. Husserl, Merleau-Ponty. Its historical and ontological relativity should be fully realized by any contemporary student of the human scene. Its cultural, socioeconomic relativity has become a commonplace among anthropologists and a platitude to the Marxists and neo-Marxists. And yet, with the consensual and interpersonal confirmation it offers, it gives us a sense of ontological security, whose validity we *experience* as self-validating, although metaphysically-historically-ontologically-socio-economically-culturally we know its apparent absolute validity as an illusion.

In fact all religious and all existential philosophies have agreed that such *egoic experience* is a preliminary illusion, a veil, a film of *maya*—a dream to Heraclitus, and to Lao Tzu, the fundamental illusion of all Buddhism, a state of sleep, of death, of socially accepted madness, a womb state to which one has to die, from which one has to be born.

The person going through ego-loss or transcendental experiences may or may not become in different ways confused. Then he might legitimately be regarded as mad. But to be mad is not necessarily to be ill, notwithstanding that in our culture the two categories have become confused. It is assumed that if a person is mad (whatever that means) then *ipso facto* he is ill (whatever that means). The experience that a person may be absorbed in, while to others he appears simply ill-mad, may be for him veritable manna from heaven. The person's whole life may be changed, but it is difficult not to doubt the validity of such vision. Also, not everyone comes back to us again.

Are these experiences simply the effulgence of a pathological process or of a particular alienation? I do not think they are.

In certain cases, a man blind from birth may have an operation performed which gives him his sight. The result—frequently misery, confusion, disorientation. The light that illumines the madman is an unearthly light. It is not always a distorted refraction of his mundane life situation. He may be irradiated by light from other worlds. It may burn him out.

This "other" world is not essentially a battlefield wherein psychological forces, derived or diverted, displaced or sublimated from their original object-cathexes, are engaged in an illusionary fight—although such forces may obscure these realities, just as they may obscure so-called external realities. When Ivan in *The Brothers Karamazov* says, "If God does not exist, everything is permissible," he is *not* saying, "If my superego, in projected form, can be abolished, I can do anything with a good conscience." He *is* saying, "If there is *only* my conscience, then there is no ultimate validity for my will."

Among physicians and priests there should be some who are guides, who can educt the person from this world and induct him to the other. To guide him in it and to lead him back again.

One enters the other world by breaking a shell: or through a door: through a partition: the curtains part or rise: a veil is lifted. Seven veils: seven seals, seven heavens.

The "ego" is the instrument for living in *this* world. If the "ego" is broken up or destroyed (by the insurmountable contradictions of certain life situations, by toxins, chemical changes, etc.), then the person may be exposed to other worlds, "real" in different ways from the more familiar territory of dreams, imagination, perception or fantasy.

The world that one enters, one's capacity to experience it, seem to be partly conditional on the state of one's "ego."

Our time has been distinguished, more than by anything else, by a drive to control the external world, and by an almost total forgetfulness of the internal world. If one estimates human evolution from the point of view of knowledge of the external world, then we are in many respects progressing.

If our estimate is from the point of view of the internal world and of oneness of internal and external, then the judgment must be very different.

Phenomenologically the terms "internal" and "external" have little validity. But in this whole realm one is reduced to mere verbal expedients —words are simply the finger pointing at the moon. One of the difficulties of talking in the present day of these matters is that the very existence of inner realities is now called in question.

By "inner" I mean our way of seeing the external world and all those realities that have no "external," "objective" presence—imagination, dreams, fantasies, trances, the realities of contemplative and meditative states, realities of which modern man, for the most part, has not the slightest direct awareness.

For example, nowhere in the Bible is there any argument about the *existence* of gods, demons, angels. People did not first "believe in" God: they experienced His presence, as was true of other spiritual agencies. The question was not whether God existed, but whether this particular God was the greatest god of all, or the only God; and what was the relation of the various spiritual agencies to each other. Today, there is a public debate, not as to the trustworthiness of God, the particular place in the spiritual hierarchy of different spirits, etc., but whether God or such spirits *even exist* or ever have existed.

Sanity today appears to rest very largely on a capacity to adapt to the external world—the interpersonal world, and the realm of human collectivities.

As this external human world is almost completely and totally estranged from the inner, any personal direct awareness of the inner world already has grave risks.

But since society, without knowing it, is *starving* for the inner, the demands on people to evoke its presence in a "safe" way, in a way that need not be taken seriously, etc., is tremendous—while the ambivalence is equally intense. Small wonder that the list of artists, in say the last 150 years, who have become shipwrecked on these reefs is so long— Hölderlin, John Clare, Rimbaud, Van Gogh, Nietzsche, Antonin Artaud. . . .

Those who survived have had exceptional qualities—a capacity for secrecy, slyness, cunning—a thoroughly realistic appraisal of the risks they run, not only from the spiritual realms they frequent, but from the hatred of their fellows for anyone engaged in this pursuit.

Let us *cure* them. The poet who mistakes a real woman for his Muse and acts accordingly. . . . The young man who sets off in a yacht in search of God. . . .

The outer divorced from any illumination from the inner is in a state of darkness. We are in an age of darkness. The state of outer darkness is a state of sin—i.e., alienation or estrangement from the *inner light.** Certain actions lead to greater estrangement; certain others help one not to be so far removed. The former used to be called sinful.

The ways of losing one's way are legion. Madness is certainly not

---

*M. Eliade, *The Two and the One* (London: Harvill Press, 1965), especially Chapter I.

the least unambiguous. The countermadness of Kraepelinian psychiatry is the exact counterpart of "official" psychosis. Literally, and absolutely seriously, it is as *mad,* if by madness we mean any radical estrangement from the totality of what is the case. Remember Kierkegaard's objective madness.

As we experience the world, so we act. We conduct ourselves in the light of our view of what is the case and what is not the case. That is, each person is a more or less naïve ontologist. Each person has views of what is and what is not.

There is no doubt, it seems to me, that there have been profound changes in the experience of man in the last thousand years. In some ways this is more evident than changes in the patterns of his behavior. There is everything to suggest that man experienced God. Faith was never a matter of believing He existed, but of trusting, in the presence that was experienced and known to exist as a self-validating datum. It seems likely that far more people in our time experience neither the presence of God, nor the presence of his absence, but the absence of his presence.

We require a history of phenomena, not simply more phenomena of history.

As it is, the secular psychotherapist is often in the role of the blind leading the half-blind.

The fountain has not played itself out, the frame still shines, the river still flows, the spring still bubbles forth, the light has not faded. But between *us* and It, there is a veil which is more like fifty feet of solid concrete. *Deus absconditus.* Or we have absconded.

Already everything in our time is directed to categorizing and segregating this reality from objective facts. This is precisely the concrete wall. Intellectually, emotionally, interpersonally, organizationally, intuitively, theoretically, we have to blast our way through the solid wall, even if at the risk of chaos, madness and death. For from *this* side of the wall, this is the risk. There are no assurances, no guarantees.

Many people are prepared to have faith in the sense of scientifically indefensible belief in an untested hypothesis. Few have trust enough to test it. Many people make-believe what they experience. Few are made to believe by their experience. Paul of Tarsus was picked up by the scruff of the neck, thrown to the ground and blinded for three days. This direct experience was self-validating.

We live in a secular world. To adapt to this world the child abdicates its ecstasy. ("*L'enfant abdique son extase*": Malarmé.) Having lost our experience of the spirit, we are expected to have faith. But this faith comes to be a belief in a reality which is not evident. There is a prophecy in Amos that a time will come when there will be a famine in the land, "not a famine for bread, nor a thirst for water, but of *hearing* the words of the Lord." That time has now come to pass. It is the present age.

From the alienated starting point of our pseudo-sanity, everything is equivocal. Our sanity is not "true" sanity. Their madness is not "true" madness. The madness of our patients is an artifact of the destruction wreaked on them by us and by them on themselves. Let no one suppose that we meet "true" madness any more than that we are truly sane. The madness that we encounter in "patients" is a gross travesty, a mockery, a grotesque caricature of what the natural healing of that estranged integration we call sanity might be. True sanity entails in one way or another the dissolution of the normal ego, that false self competently adjusted to our alienated social reality; the emergence of the "inner" archetypal mediators of divine power, and through this death a rebirth, and the eventual re-establishment of a new kind of ego-functioning, the ego now being the servant of the divine, no longer its betrayer.

It

Alan W. Watts

Is there in any of us an instinct to get "outside" of our own physical being? Is there a justification for escape, for getting away from it all? Alan W. Watts thinks so. Man has a need to relate himself to something outside, something other, something Watts calls "It."

The history of man includes far too many references to mysticism and transcendent experiences for today's behavioral scientist to ignore this area, troublesome and unempirical as it may seem.

Excerpts from pp. 128—129, 131—133, 135—143 from *The Book: On the Taboo Against Knowing Who You Are*, by Alan W. Watts. Copyright © 1966 by Alan Watts. Reprinted by permission of Pantheon Books, a Division of Random House, Inc.

The Book: On the Taboo Against Knowing Who You Are is one of Watts' varied attempts to help Western man to know the larger self. Again, you are invited to explore this area and make up your own mind.

Just as true humor is laughter at oneself, true humanity is knowledge of oneself. Other creatures may love and laugh, talk and think, but it seems to be the special peculiarity of human beings that they reflect: they think about thinking and know that they know. This, like other feedback systems, may lead to vicious circles and confusions if improperly managed, but self-awareness makes human experience resonant. It imparts that simultaneous "echo" to all that we think and feel as the box of a violin reverberates with the sound of the strings. It gives depth and volume to what would otherwise be shallow and flat.

Self-knowledge leads to wonder, and wonder to curiosity and investigation, so that nothing interests people more than people, even if only one's own person. Every intelligent individual wants to know what makes him tick, and yet is at once fascinated and frustrated by the fact that oneself is the most difficult of all things to know. For the human organism is, apparently, the most complex of all organisms, and while one has the advantage of knowing one's own organism so intimately—from the inside—there is also the disadvantage of being so close to it that one can never quite get at it. Nothing so eludes conscious inspection as consciousness itself. This is why the root of consciousness has been called, paradoxically, the unconscious.

The people we are tempted to call clods and boors are just those who seem to find nothing fascinating in being human; their humanity is incomplete, for it has never astonished them. There is also something incomplete about those who find nothing fascinating in *being*. You may say that this is a philosopher's professional prejudice—that people are defective who lack a sense of the metaphysical. But anyone who thinks at all must be a philosopher—a good one or a bad one—because it is impossible to think without premises, without basic (and in this sense, metaphysical) assumptions about what is sensible, what is the good life, what is beauty, and what is pleasure. To hold such assumptions, consciously or unconsciously, is to philosophize. The self-styled practical man of affairs who pooh-poohs philosophy as a lot of windy notions is himself a pragmatist or a positivist, and a bad one at that, since he has given no thought to his position.

If the human organism is fascinating, the environment which accompanies it is equally so—and not merely as a collection of particular things and events. Chemistry, biology, geology, and astronomy are special fascinations with the details of our environment, but metaphysics is fascination with the whole thing. I find it almost impossible to imagine a sensitive human being bereft of metaphysical wonder, a person who does not have that marvelous urge to ask a question that cannot quite be formulated. If, as we have been arguing, the only real atom—as de Chardin put it—is the universe, and the only real thing is everything, then what is it?

Yet the moment I have asked this question, I must question the question. What sort of answer could such a question have? Ordinarily, one answers the question "What is it?" by putting the designated thing or event into a class—animal, vegetable, or mineral, solid, liquid, or gas, running, jumping, or walking. But what class will fit *every*thing? What can possibly be said about everything? To define is to limit, to set boundaries, to compare and to contrast, and for this reason the universe, the all, seems to defy definition. At this point, the mind runs into an apparently absolute limitation, and one may well argue that it is therefore a misuse of the mind to ask such a question. Just as no one in his senses would look for the morning news in a dictionary, no one should use speaking and thinking to find out what cannot be spoken or thought. Logically, then, the question "What is everything?" has no meaning, even though it seems to be profound. As Wittgenstein suggested, people who ask such questions may have a disorder of the intellect which can be cured by philosophical therapy. To "do philosophy," as he put it, is to think about thinking in such a way that we can distinguish real thinking from nonsense.

But this neat logic does not get rid of the urge to know which expresses itself—however ineptly—in the question. As I said at the beginning, it is just unbelievably odd that anything is happening at all. Yet how am I to express this feeling in the form of a sensible question which could have a satisfactory answer? The point is, perhaps, that I am not looking for a *verbal* answer, just as when I ask for a kiss, I do not want a piece of paper with "A kiss" written on it. It is rather that metaphysical wonder looks for an experience, a vision, a revelation which will explain, without words, why there is the universe, and what it is—much as the act of loving explains why we are male and female.

It could be said, then, that the best answer to "What is everything?" is "Look and see!" But the question almost always implies a search for something *basic* to everything, for an underlying unity which our ordinary thinking and feeling do not grasp. Thought and sensation are analytical and selective, and thus present the world as no more than a multiplicity of things and events. Man has, however, a "metaphysical instinct" which apparent multiplicity does not satisfy.

> What guarantee is there that the five senses, taken together, do cover the whole of possible experience? They cover simply our actual experience, our human knowledge of facts or events. There are gaps between the fingers; there are gaps between the senses. In these gaps is the darkness which hides the connection between things. . . . This darkness is the source of our vague fears and anxieties, but also the home of the gods. They alone see the connections, the total relevance of everything that happens; that which now comes to us in bits and pieces, the "accidents" which exist only in our heads, in our limited perceptions.[1]

Man is therefore intuitively certain that the entire multitude of things and events is "on" or "in" something as reflections are on a mirror, sounds on a diaphragm, lights and colors in a diamond, or the words and music of a song in the singer. This is perhaps because man is himself a unified organism, and that if things and events are "on" anything at all, they are on his nervous system. Yet there is obviously more than one nervous system, and what are all nervous systems on? Each other?

This mysterious something has been called God, the Absolute, Nature, Substance, Energy, Space, Ether, Mind, Being, the Void, the Infinite—names and ideas which shift in popularity and respectability with the winds of intellectual fashion, of considering the universe intelligent or stupid, superhuman or subhuman, specific or vague. All of them might be dismissed as nonsense-noises if the notion of an underlying Ground of Being were no more than a product of intellectual speculation. But these names are often used to designate the content of a vivid and almost sensorily concrete experience—the "unitive" experience of the mystic, which, with secondary variations, is found in almost all cultures

---

1. Idris Parry, "Kafka, Rilke, and Rumpelstiltskin." *The Listener*. British Broadcasting Corporation, London, December 2, 1965, p. 895.

at all times. This experience is the transformed sense of self which I was discussing in the previous chapter, though in "naturalistic" terms, purified of all hocus-pocus about mind, soul, spirit, and other intellectually gaseous words.

Despite the universality of this experience and the impressive regularity with which it is described in the same general way,[2] tough-minded types regard it as a commonly recurring hallucination with characteristic symptoms, like paranoia, which adds nothing to our information about the physical universe. Just as we cannot say anything about everything, so, they argue, one cannot feel or experience anything about everything. For all our senses are selective. We experience by contrast just as we think by contrast. To experience something underlying *all* experiences would thus be like seeing sight itself, as something common to everything seen. In terms of what color, what shape—other than all mutually contrasting colors and shapes—could we see sight itself? . . .

But the underlying assumption, that all knowledge is in terms of contrasts, is as metaphysical as an assumption can be. Put it in another way: "All knowledge is a recognition of the mutual relations between sense-experiences and/or things and events." This comes perilously close to being a meaningful statement about everything. "All things are known by their differences from the likenesses to each other." Backed up into this position, the antimetaphysician can be carried, albeit with screams of protest, to an even deeper metaphysical level. . . .

I have sometimes thought that all philosophical disputes could be reduced to an argument between the partisans of "prickles" and the partisans of "goo." The prickly people are tough-minded, rigorous, and precise, and like to stress differences and divisions between things. They prefer particles to waves, and discontinuity to continuity. The gooey people are tender-minded romanticists who love wide generalizations and grand syntheses. They stress the underlying unities, and are inclined to pantheism and mysticism. Waves suit them much better than particles as the ultimate constituents of matter, and discontinuities jar their teeth like a compressed-air drill. Prickly philosophers consider the gooey ones

---

2. For which the reader is directed to such works as Bucke's *Cosmic Consciousness,* James's *Varieties of Religious Experience,* and Johnson's *Watcher on the Hills.*

rather disgusting—undisciplined, vague dreamers who slide over hard facts like an intellectual slime which threatens to engulf the whole universe in an "undifferentiated aesthetic continuum" (courtesy of Professor F. S. C. Northrop). But gooey philosophers think of their prickly colleagues as animated skeletons that rattle and click without any flesh or vital juices, as dry and dessicated mechanisms bereft of all finer feelings. Either party would be hopelessly lost without the other, because there would be nothing to argue about, no one would know what his position was, and the whole course of philosophy would come to an end.

As things now stand in the world of academic philosophy, the prickly people have had the upper hand in both England and the United States for some years. With their penchant for linguistic analysis, mathematical logic, and scientific empiricism, they have aligned philosophy with the mystique of science, have begun to transform the philosopher's library or mountain retreat into something nearer to a laboratory, and, as William Earle said, would come to work in white coats if they thought they could get away with it. The professional journals are now as satisfactorily unreadable as treatises on mathematical physics, and the points at issue as minute as any animalcule in the biologist's microscope. But their sweeping victory over the gooey people has almost abolished philosophy as a discipline, for we are close to the point where departments of philosophy will close their offices and shift the remaining members of their faculties to the departments of mathematics and linguistics. . . .

To go anywhere in philosophy, other than back and forth, round and round, one must have a keen sense of *correlative vision*. This is a technical term for a thorough understanding of the Game of Black-and-White, whereby one sees that all explicit opposites are implicit allies—correlative in the sense that they "gowith" each other and cannot exist apart. This, rather than any miasmic absorption of differences into a continuum of ultimate goo, is the metaphysical unity underlying the world. For this unity is not mere one-ness as opposed to multiplicity, since these two terms are themselves polar. The unity, or inseparability, of one and many is therefore referred to in Vedanta philosophy as "non-duality" (*advaita*) to distinguish it from simple uniformity. True, the term has its own opposite, "duality," for insofar as every term designates a class, an intellectual pigeonhole, every class has an outside polarizing its inside. For this reason, language can no more transcend duality than painting or photographs upon a flat surface can go beyond two dimensions. Yet by the convention of perspective, certain two-dimensional lines that slant towards a "vanishing-point" are taken to represent the third dimension of depth. In a similar way, the dualistic term "non-duality" is taken to represent the "dimension" in which explicit differences have implicit unity. . . .

Is it possible that myself, my existence, so *contains* being and nothing that death is merely the "off" interval in an on/off pulsation which must be eternal—because every alternative to this pulsation (e.g., its absence) would in due course imply its presence? Is it conceivable, then, that I am basically an eternal existence momentarily and perhaps needlessly terrified by one half of itself because it has identified all of itself with the other half? If the choice must be either white or black, must I so commit myself to the white side that I cannot be a good sport and actually play the Game of Black-and-White, with the implicit knowledge that neither can win? Or is all this so much bandying with the formal relations between words and terms without any relation to my physical situation?

To answer the last question affirmatively, I should have to believe that the logic of thought is quite arbitrary—that it is a purely and strictly human invention without any basis in the physical universe. While it is true, as I have already shown, that we do project logical patterns (nets, grids, and other types of calculus) upon the wiggly physical world—which can be confusing if we do not realize what we are doing—nevertheless, these patterns do not come from *outside* the world. They have something to do with the design of the human nervous system, which is definitely in and of the world. Furthermore, I have shown that correlative thinking about the relation of organism to environment is far more compatible with the physical sciences than our archaic and prevalent notions of the self as something confronting an alien and separate world. To sever the connections between human logic and the physical universe. I would have to revert to the myth of the ego as an isolated, independent observer from whom the rest of the world is absolutely external and "other." Neither neurology nor biology nor sociology can subscribe to this.

If, on the other hand, self and other, subject and object, organism and environment are the poles of a single process, THAT is my true existence. As the *Upanishads* say, "That is the Self. That is the real. That are thou!" But I cannot think or say anything about THAT, or, as I shall now call it, IT unless I resort to the convention of using dualistic language as the lines of perspective are used to show depth on a flat surface. What lies beyond opposites must be discussed, if at all, in terms of opposites, and this means using the language of analogy, metaphor, and myth.

The difficulty is not only that language is dualistic, insofar as words are labels for mutually exclusive classes. The problem is that IT is so much more myself than I thought I was, so central and so basic to my existence, that I cannot make it an object. There is no way to stand outside IT, and, in fact, no need to do so. For so long as I am trying to grasp IT, I am implying that IT is not really myself. If it were possible, I am losing the sense of it by attempting to find it. This is why those who really know that they are IT invariably say they do not understand it, for IT understands understanding—not the other way about. One cannot, and need not, go deeper than deep!

But the fact that IT eludes every description must not, as happens so often, be mistaken for the description of IT as the airiest of abstractions, as a literal transparent continuum or undifferentiated cosmic jello. The most concrete image of God the Father, with his white beard and golden robe, is better than that. Yet Western students of Eastern philosophies and religions persistently accuse Hindus and Buddhists of believing in a featureless and gelatinous God, just because the latter insist that every conception or objective image of IT is void. But the term "void" applies to all such conceptions, not to IT. . . .

You were probably brought up in a culture where the presiding image of IT has for centuries been God the Father, whose pronoun is He, because IT seems too impersonal and She would, of course, be inferior. Is this image still workable, as a functional myth to provide some consensus about life and its meaning for all the diverse peoples and cultures of this planet?

Frankly, the image of God the Father has become ridiculous—that is, unless you read Saint Thomas Aquinas or Martin Buber or Paul Tillich, and realize that you can be a devout Jew or Christian without having to believe, literally, in the Cosmic Male Parent. Even then, it is difficult not to feel the force of the image, because images sway our emotions more deeply than conceptions. As a devout Christian you would be saying day after day the prayer, "Our Father who art in heaven," and eventually it gets you: you are relating emotionally to IT as to an idealized father—male, loving but stern, and a personal being quite other than yourself. Obviously, you must be other than God so long as you conceive yourself as the separate ego, but when we realize that this form of identity is no more than a social institution, and one which has ceased to be a workable life-game, the sharp division between oneself and the ultimate reality is no longer relevant.

Furthermore, the younger members of our society have for some time been in growing rebellion against paternal authority and the paternal state. For one reason, the home in an industrial society is chiefly a dormitory, and the father does not work there, with the result that wife and children have no part in his vocation. He is just a character who brings in money, and after working hours he is supposed to forget about his job and have fun. Novels, magazines, television, and popular cartoons therefore portray "Dad" as an incompetent clown. And the image has some truth in it because Dad has fallen for the hoax that work is simply something you do to make money, and with money you can get anything you want.

It is no wonder that an increasing proportion of college students want no part in Dad's world, and will do anything to avoid the rat-race of the salesman, commuter, clerk and corporate executive. Professional men, too—architects, doctors, lawyers, ministers, and professors—have offices away from home, and thus, because the demands of their families boil down more and more to money, are ever more tempted to regard even professional vocations as ways of making money. All this is further aggravated by the fact that parents no longer educate their own children. Thus the child does not grow up with understanding of or enthusiasm for his father's work. Instead, he is sent to an understaffed school run mostly by women which, under the circumstances, can do no more than hand out mass-produced education which prepares the child for everything and nothing. It has no relation whatever to his father's vocation....

Hitherto the poets and philosophers of science have used the vast expanse and duration of the universe as a pretext for reflections on the unimportance of man, forgetting that man with "that enchanted loom, the brain" is precisely what transforms this immense electrical pulsation into light and color, shape and sound, large and small, hard and heavy, long and short. In knowing the world we humanize it, and if, as we discover it, we are astonished at its dimensions and its complexity, we should be just as astonished that we have the brains to perceive it.

Hitherto we have been taught, however, that we are not really responsible for our brains. We do not know (in terms of words or figures) how they are constructed, and thus it seems that the brain and the organism as a whole are an ingenious vehicle which has been "given" to us, or an uncanny maze in which we are temporarily trapped. In other words, we accepted a definition of ourselves which confined the self to the source and to the limitations of conscious attention. This definition is miserably insufficient, for in fact we know how to grow brains and eyes, ears and fingers, hearts and bones, in just the same way that we know how to walk and breathe, talk and think—only we can't put it into words. Words are too slow and too clumsy for describing such things, and conscious attention is too narrow for keeping track of all their details.

Thus it will often happen that when you tell a girl how beautiful she is, she will say, "Now isn't that just like a man! All you men think about is bodies. OK, so I'm beautiful, but I got my body from my parents and it was just luck. I prefer to be admired for myself, not my chassis." Poor little chauffeur! All she is saying is that she has lost touch with her own astonishing wisdom and ingenuity, and wants to be admired for some trivial tricks that she can perform with her conscious attention. And we are all in the same situation, having dissociated ourselves from our bodies and from the whole network of forces in which bodies can come to birth and live.

Yet we can still awaken the sense that all this, too, is the self—a self, however, which is far beyond the image of the ego, or of the human body as limited by the skin. We then behold the Self wherever we look, and its image is the universe in its light and in its darkness, in its bodies and in its spaces. This is the new image of man, but it is still an image. For there remains—to use dualistic words—"behind," "under," "encompassing," and "central" to it all the unthinkable IT, polarizing itself in the visible contrasts of waves and troughs, solids and spaces. But the odd thing is that this IT, however inconceivable, is no vapid abstraction: it is very simply and truly yourself.

In the words of a Chinese Zen master, "Nothing is left to you at this moment but to have a good laugh!" As James Broughton put it:

This is It
and I am It
and You are It
and so is That
and He is It
and She is It
and It is It
and That is That.[4]

True humor is, indeed, laughter at one's Self—at the Divine Comedy, the fabulous deception, whereby one comes to imagine that a creature *in* existence is not also *of* existence, that what man is is not also what everything is. All the time we "know it in our bones" but conscious attention, distracted by details and differences, cannot see the whole for the parts.

The major trick in this deception is, of course, death. Consider death as the permanent end of consciousness, the point at which you and your knowledge of the universe simply cease, and where you become as if you had never existed at all. Consider it also on a much vaster scale—the death of the universe at the time when all energy runs out, when, according to some cosmologists, the explosion which flung the galaxies into space fades out like a skyrocket. It will be as if it had never happened, which is, of course, the way things were before it *did* happen. Likewise, when you are dead, you will be as you were before you were conceived. So—there has been a flash, a flash of consciousness or a flash of galaxies. It happened. Even if there is no one left to remember. . . .

I presume, then, that with my own death I shall forget who I was, just as my conscious attention is unable to recall, if it ever knew, how to form the cells of the brain and the pattern of the veins. Conscious memory plays little part in our biological existence. Thus as my sensation of "I-ness," of being alive, once came into being without conscious memory or intent, so it will arise again and again, as the "central" Self—the IT—appears as the self/other situation in its myriads of pulsating forms—always the same and always new, a here in the midst of a there, a now in the midst of then, and one in the midst of many. And if I

---

4. From *The Bard and the Harper,* recorded by James Broughton and Joel Andrews. LP–1013, produced by Musical Engineering Associates, Sausalito, California, 1965.

forget how many times I have been here, and in how many shapes, this forgetting is the necessary interval of darkness between every pulsation of light. I return in every baby born.

Actually, we know this already. After people die, babies are born—and, unless they are automata, every one of them is, just as we ourselves, were, the "I" experience coming again into being. The conditions of heredity and environment change, but each of those babies incarnates the same experience of being central to a world that is "other." Each infant dawns into life as I did, without any memory of a past. Thus when I am gone there can be no experience, no living through, of the state of being a perpetual "has-been." Nature "abhors the vacuum" and the I-feeling appears again as it did before, and it matters not whether the interval be ten seconds or billions of years. In unconsciousness all times are the same brief instant.

This is so obvious, but our block against seeing it is the ingrained and compelling myth that the "I" comes into this world, or is thrown out from it, in such a way as to have no essential connection with it. Thus we do not trust the universe to repeat what it has already done—to "I" itself again and again. We see it as an eternal arena in which the individual is no more than a temporary stranger—a visitor who hardly belongs—for the thin ray of consciousness does not shine upon its own source. In looking out upon the world, we forget that the world is looking at itself—through our eyes and IT's.

Now you know—even if it takes you some time to do a double-take and get the full impact. It may not be easy to recover from the many generations through which the fathers have knocked down the children, like dominoes, saying, "Don't you dare think that thought! You're just a little upstart, just a creature, and you had better learn your place." On the contrary, you're IT. But perhaps the fathers were unwittingly trying to tell the children that IT plays IT cool. You don't come on (that is, on stage) like IT because you really are IT, and the point of the stage is to show on, not to show off. To come on like IT—to play at being God—is to play the Self as a role, which is just what it isn't. When IT plays, it plays at being everything else.

The Loving Self

Love is the final word. Having said it, you've said it all. The self is what emerges as a person knows and loves himself. He experiences himself and expresses himself most fully in the love relationship.

To the millions of words that have been written about love in any one year, what can we hope to add? We haven't attempted anything so grandiose. We have attempted only to portray some of the deepest meanings of love.

Marshall Hodge is a psychologist in private practice in Claremont, California. He is the author of *Your Fear of Love,* a sensitive and lucid presentation of what love is all about.

John Brennecke is also a psychologist. In his teaching and clinical work, he has experienced some of the satisfactions of seeing "love in action," especially in the learning of the fuller meanings of love. He is co-editor of this volume.

Loving and Trembling

Marshall B. Hodge

Why do we avoid each other? Why do people shy away from closeness and intimacy? Are there secret fears that keep us from loving? How do we recognize love and how do we root out the obstacles that interfere with our fullest appreciation of each other?

Doctor Marshall B. Hodge offers us some of his deeper insights, gleaned from his practice of psychotherapy and marriage counseling. We must love in order to be full and free persons. Yet many of us don't love, either because we don't know how or are afraid to try.

Ted, a man in his middle twenties, sought the help of a psychotherapist because he was having difficulty in his marriage. One week, after he had had several sessions with the therapist, sudden and dramatic changes occurred in his relationship with his wife, Patti.

Both of them began to talk to each other about events and feelings that they had never discussed before. In some ways it was an agonizing week for them. Anger that had been pent up for months, and even years, poured forth. In the course of their self-disclosures each of them revealed that they had had brief sexual "flings" with another since their marriage. More expressions of anger and hurt burst forth, reaching an intensity they had never experienced before. But when the anger and hurt had been expressed other feelings began to manifest themselves. They became aware that they felt closer and more sexually alive to each other than they ever had before. As they moved toward each other they found themselves exquisitely sensitive to each other's touches and caresses.

Sexual intercourse had always been marred for the couple by the fact that Ted invariably had his orgasm almost immediately after entering the vagina, leaving both Patti and himself feeling frustrated and cheated. Now, suddenly, this, too, was changed. To his amazement he found that during intercourse he now remained for many minutes at the peak of the most delicious sexual enjoyment he had ever experienced, yet he was not aware of making any effort to control the timing of his sexual climax, but was caught up completely in the enjoyment of his own sensations and Patti's obvious enjoyment.

All of this occurred in one week between Ted's sessions with the therapist. When he appeared for his next hour it was natural that he describe what had happened. He did so with great enthusiasm, but then he said, "It was such a great week that I just can't understand what happened to me today. I discovered that my hands were literally shaking, and I just felt scared to death."

Ted's bewilderment was understandable. He assumed that he would feel more confident because of his new-found ability to be more completely himself and more expressive of his love and his sexual desire. The last thing he expected of himself was that he would become very frightened. He did not reckon with his fear of love, which he has in common with the rest of us.

Time and again experiences such as this confirm that we are most frightened by that for which we most long—the experience of intimacy. What can we do about this fear of love, which so often confronts us in ourselves and in those we love?

Perhaps one of the most helpful things we can do about it is to become clearly aware of it. Our relationships would often be more understandable if we could see these fears clearly in ourselves and others. For example, couples frequently report sequences of events in which they first felt very close and then shortly thereafter began arguing or nagging one another about some seemingly insignificant thing. These experiences mystify them and often lead to doubts about their love for each other. It would be helpful if we could recognize that for most of us the exquisite experience of intimacy is a razor's edge, which we cannot allow to exist for more than a few moments. When intimacy does occur, then we frequently trump up some "reason" for moving away from it.

In other instances we prevent ourselves from even momentary experiences of intimacy by finding something (almost anything!) to be angry, hurt, irritated, nervous, or busy about any time love comes threateningly close.

Anna, a woman in her early forties who was seeing a psychotherapist, followed a constant pattern for many weeks in her sessions. It would often be obvious during her weekly hour that she had some inclination to respond to the feelings of warmth and acceptance that he felt for her. Invariably, however, toward the end of the session she would find some reason to become violently angry with him. She would read some manipulative or rejecting meaning into some innocuous statement or glance of his. She would then explode at him, accuse him of being a phony and a charlatan, and stomp out of the room after hurling all manner of invectives at him. On one occasion when she was angry she refused to leave; and it was necessary for him to call the police to force her to do so.

But some dogged persistence in Anna kept her coming back week after week. And despite the anger that her behavior aroused in the therapist, which frequently led him to shout back and threaten never to see her again, he allowed the appointments to continue. Finally, after the pattern of her behavior had been pointed out many times, Anna gradually became aware of the fact that she was desperately frightened of caring. She began to recognize that she had to reject and hurt anyone who gave evidence of caring for her lest she be caught in the trap of the vulnerability of caring and be hurt again as she had been hurt many times before. Once this awareness began to dawn on her, Anna's moments of anger toward the therapist became less frequent, less violent, and more quickly over and done with when they did occur.

Gaining awareness of our fear of love is often a difficult task, for we tend to disguise it from ourselves and others by employing many defenses against intimacy.

One man, Bill, invariably sounded angry in any discussion with his wife. The two of them had been seeing a marriage counselor together for a number of sessions. During these sessions the two of them often clashed, and the arguments frequently seemed to start because Bill sounded so angry. Finally the therapist became suspicious of this, and when the husband spoke out loudly and with apparent anger toward his wife, the therapist interrupted to ask, "Bill, are you really angry right now?" Bill replied that he was not. "You sound as though you are." To this remark Bill replied, "I'm just speaking positively and with conviction. I'm not mad."

It appeared on further exploration that Bill was often not angry when he sounded as though he were. Perhaps he did have a reservoir of hostility built up over the years that had something to do with this behavior, but the function that it appeared to serve in relation to his wife and other people he cared for was one of keeping it virtually impossible to experience intimacy.

There are many similar defenses against intimacy. We may keep people at a distance by seeming indifferent to them, by being rigid or legalistic, or by playing the role of martyr. As long as we are successful at employing these ways of keeping others away, it is hard for us to become aware of our fear of love, for we make the possibility of intimacy so remote that there is little "danger" of our experiencing it. With the lion so successfully caged, we do not become aware of our fear of it!

Recognizing Our Fear of Love

If we can begin to see what we are doing and begin to give up some of our defenses, then we will be more likely to experience our fear of love directly. Once this occurs we are in a much better position to do something about it. It will also be helpful if we cannot only be aware of our fear of love, but also accept it both in ourselves and in others. Here, as elsewhere, caring for ourselves seems to be the starting point for personality growth.

If we can experience and accept our fear of love, we will have less need of indirect ways of expressing it, which are almost invariably harmful to relationships. Instead of finding some pretext for withdrawing when we experience more intimacy than our fear will permit, we can admit our fear to ourselves and often to the other person as well. This direct way of responding to our fear will be far less destructive to the relationship. A natural ebb and flow of the experience and expression of love will then be possible, as we experience such intimacy as we are ready for and then withdraw for a time as our fear asserts itself too strongly. As we see this pattern clearly we will be far more able to take in stride apparent setbacks in our associations with others.

It also makes a big difference when we can recognize that when someone we love acts destructively or hurtfully toward us it is almost certainly an indication that he, too, is afraid rather than that he does not care for us. We may be just as hurt or express as much anger as we would if we did not have this insight. The chances of resolving the situation are much better, however, because we ourselves will not be likely to react as though we have been completely rejected and unloved. This is when we often play that "he loves me, he loves me not" game in which we tally up what we consider to be indications of how the other person feels about us. Often our feelings of worth become involved, as we say to ourselves, "There must be something the matter with me or he wouldn't treat me this way."

This game is pointless, for the problem does not usually lie in the absence of caring but rather in the fear of love, which leads the person to act as though he does not care. Of course, recognizing the existence of the fear of love does not always lead to a resolution of interpersonal difficulties. A woman, for example, might see that her husband belittles her constantly as a means of avoiding intimacy and as a way of coping with his own self-hate. Yet if she saw no crack in the wall of this defense, she might ultimately come to the conclusion that it would be self-destructive for her to continue the marriage. And a child might still have to be taken from a cruel father even though it might be recognized that his brutality is rooted in a terrible fear of love.

It will also be helpful if we can discover that the potential hurt of not experiencing and expressing love ultimately far outweighs the risks that accompany intimacy. We can never eliminate the possibility that we will be hurt when we dare to love. The emotional involvement of caring always includes vulnerability; in fact we can be certain that we will sometimes be hurt if we allow ourselves to love. Someone we love will die; someone we love will be injured; someone we love will be incurably and painfully ill; someone we love will be so frightened and mistrustful of our caring that they will react in ways that are hurtful or even destructive to us.

These are painful experiences, and we cannot avoid them if we choose to love. It is part of the human dilemma that love always includes the element of hurt. We are invariably hurt by those we love, and, as the song has it, "You always hurt the one you love, the one you shouldn't hurt at all." So it is not surprising that we are frightened of love and tend to shy away from it. The self-disclosure and involvement of love is a sometimes painful joy.

What are the alternatives to a life in which love is experienced and expressed? Does such a life hold out the hope of any less hurt? Only two other alternatives appear to be available. One would be, if it is possible, to cut oneself off completely from the experience of love. Such a person would say in effect to themselves, "I won't allow anyone to mean anything to me. I may have business relationships of one kind or another, but no one will be important to me beyond the immediate dealings in which we find each other useful, and no one will learn any-thing of a personal nature about how I feel or who I really am. I'll never allow myself to experience the desire or need for love." Perhaps this kind of life could be achieved, but it sounds like a desperately lonely existence. Perhaps a person could keep so busy or be so controlled that he could even block the loneliness out of awareness, but what kind of life is that? The viewpoint suggested here does, of course, involve a value judgment that meaningfulness is found above all else in human relationships, although it does appear that few of us would *choose* to live so isolated an existence.

The other alternative is more often practiced, but is seems almost equally unsatisfying. This way of life would be to love guardedly and almost secretly. Although he may not be aware of it, such a person says to himself, "All right, so I admit *to myself* that I care for my children and my wife. And maybe there are a few other people in the world who mean something to me. But I'm going to play it cool. I'll never reveal too much of myself or let them know how much I care. No sense getting too far out on a limb or being too enthusiastic about our relationship. No use letting them see how much they mean to me. They'd be likely to find some way of using it to push me around or hurt me." A lot of us settle for this approach to love. But this, too, makes for a kind of loneliness and cheats us out of the deepest and most satisfying experi-ences of love. And since it involves a guardedness and calculated dullness in our relationships, it cheats us of the free, unburdened feeling that spontaneity in our actions and words could give us. All of life becomes toned down and the exhilarating excitement is taken away.

The risks of love are ever-present, but the alternatives are not inviting. So from the standpoint of satisfying living it *is* better even "to have loved and lost than never to have loved at all."

Taking a Chance on Love

If we postponed the experience and expression of love until we no longer feared it, we would postpone it forever. Some people do appear to use their fear of love as a perpetual excuse for stalemated living—loving and trembling seem to go together. If we desire love we must learn to love in spite of our fears.

This process of "taking a chance on love" might be compared to the experience of a person who wants to make parachute jumps. If he is not a fool, he is frightened. And no amount of prejump training will eradicate that fear. When the time comes to make the leap he will be trembling internally and, quite possibly, externally. No amount of reassurance by experienced jumpers will make it otherwise. Making the leap of love is not too unlike this. No amount of advance preparation or reassurance from others will keep us from experiencing fear. It is different, however, in that we can make some tentative leaps in the direction of self-disclosure and the involvement of love and withdraw back into the security of emotional distance if the experience is too frightening. The parachutist, once committed, doesn't have that option!

When we make our first moves toward deeper experiences and more open expressions of love, it may seem at first that our fear is greatly intensified. This is a very critical time, for we may become so frightened that we choose to withdraw permanently and not allow ourselves another chance to feel so deeply.

This sometimes happens in psychotherapy. After a few sessions a person may begin to respond to the therapist's warmth with feelings of caring. Perhaps the individual does not even allow himself to verbalize these feelings but suddenly "discovers" he cannot afford the sessions or does not have sufficient time to work them into a busy schedule.

It is understandable that the experience of fear is intensified at first when we allow ourselves to love more deeply. In the past our defenses —the devices we used to keep ourselves emotionally distant from others —protected us not only from the experience of love but also from the full awareness of our fear. As we allow the defenses to crumble we stand naked and vulnerable before our fear.

One thing that will help as we begin to allow ourselves the experience of love will be the awareness that we are no longer in the same circumstances as we were when the fear developed within us. When we were first exposed to the risks of love, we were children. And when we experienced the hurts of feeling rejected, we were relatively helpless to do anything about the situation. No wonder we were frightened and built whatever defenses against hurt we could by walling ourselves off emotionally.

We Aren't Helpless

Often as adults we still feel helpless, as though we were still children. But we are not helpless. If we express love and are rejected, we can do something about it—we can express our anger and frustration. If our loving proves unsatisfying we can withdraw from that person if we choose to and express our love to others more able to respond. We can also discover that another person's inability to express love to us when we love them has nothing to do with our value as a person. Perhaps most important of all we can learn that we can survive hurt and that, while it is never pleasant, it need not be catastrophic.

Our fear of love will never completely disappear any more than would the fear of the parachutist. In both instances there is always a realistic risk of hurt, but as we are able to enter into more and more emotionally intimate relationships, the fear will gradually lessen. We will learn from experience that the satisfactions far exceed the occasional hurts we experience, and we will have so much fun enjoying the intimacy and the freedom of spontaneous living, we will give decreasing attention to the hurts or our fear of them.

We will find it increasingly easy to be ourselves and to express all our feelings, for we will have increasing confidence that people will generally like us as we are. And when we are frightened, we will likely find it comfortable to express that feeling, too—and expressing it will help to dissipate it.

A sentence in the New Testament reads, "There is no fear in love, but perfect love casts out fear." (I John 4:18) It is true. There is no fear *in* love—only fear *of* love and the vulnerability it involves. And the repeated experience of love reduces fear.

Whether the central message of the New Testament, which revolves around the crucifixion of Jesus, is regarded as the literal truth or as a myth growing out of man's yearning for meaning in life, the theme is a deeply moving one. It is often garbled by theological lingo, but it finally comes down to relationships and appears to be essentially this: God risked creating persons so independent they could love him or thumb their noses at him. He went even further and chose to love them. As it always does, the decision to love necessarily included suffering. But it must have been worth the risk, for perhaps the alternative even for God was the ultimate loneliness of having no one to love.

We can discover for ourselves that it is worth the risk to love, even though we tremble and even though we know we will sometimes experience the hurt we fear.

The Mysteries of Love

John H. Brennecke

There are lots of things written about love. Love's ecstasies, agonies, highs, lows, ins and outs, all are extolled by writers of every kind, in every language, from every land. The most used (and abused) word is still the least understood concept.

Love is a mystery and contains many other mysteries. The following article, written especially for this book, attempts to describe some of these mysterious properties of love. The author, a psychologist and college teacher, has been engaged in marriage and family counseling and psychotherapy for the past eight years. Throughout his work, Mr. Brennecke has attempted to show people that love is still one of the most important and productive things man has going for him. When everything else has failed, we still have love to try. Most of us don't really try it.

Most of us don't love. This isn't a statement designed to stir up controversy or stimulate debate: it's a statement of information. I don't pretend to be wise. I claim a certain intelligence, a bit of practical knowledge, a smattering of common sense. But I have not yet lived fully enough to claim wisdom. What I am claiming in my opening sentence is a beginning of wisdom.

Many of us lust. We can, most of us, stir up enough animal drive and physical power to seek, find, and consummate a physical erotic experience.

Many of us feel desire. Almost any healthy person can know what it feels like to want to be with someone, to touch and hold and experience him fully. We also can know what it's like to be desired. That feels nice. You can go all day on that feeling.

Many of us know affection. We can pat and touch, hug and kiss, nuzzle and snuggle, grip and grapple: it's fun, and nearly everyone enjoys it. It feels good to get it and it also feels very nice to give it.

Many of us enjoy the company of another person, or many others.

Written especially for this anthology by John H. Brennecke.

This involves shared interests, shared symbols (like words and ideas), and some emotions that we can have in common.

Many of us feel good about another person. We appreciate him, value him, like him, enjoy him (possibly, though who's to say this is a necessity?), or want to express some kind of good feeling about him.

Many people feel respect for others, too. They stand in some kind of awe or reverence, possibly, or maybe just a simple feeling of deference.

But, these things, whatever else they are, don't really qualify as love. Why not?

The reasons are complex, but they *can* be described. Most of us don't really know what love is. Many people claim to love, to be in love, to write on, preach about, teach about, or counsel in, love. But if my own life and loving tells me anything, it's that love is a "sweet, elusive butterfly," as the song says.

Love is a fragile and intangible "something." Like Zen, "that which can be expressed in words *isn't*" love. This smacks of mysticism and fantasy. Possibly there is a lot of both involved in love. Certainly what Dr. Harlow calls "love" when he writes about the need for contact comfort in his monkeys isn't all there is to it. Certainly, the moods and emotions sung about, poetized about, and dreamed about aren't all there is to it.

Erich Fromm tells us that to really experience love you must *trust* the loved one. Trust, or the willingness to put yourself into the keeping of someone else, is a fairly rare commodity today. We are into a mood of distrust and skepticism. We are caught up in a form of suspiciousness and social distance that really makes trust seem like a naïve, and therefore, impractical, behavior, Trusting people, we're told, get caught, used, taken advantage of, and they certainly stand a damned good chance of getting hurt. Moreover, they lose. We live in a society that worships winning, achieving. Losers are scorned, pitied, spit on, and relegated to the cellar, whether in baseball ("nice guys finish last") or business ("dog eats dog in this game, Charlie!"), or politics.

Nonetheless, trust we must, or love just doesn't happen. If we're going to take this matter of loving seriously, then we may just have to take the risky course of trusting. You must be willing to "put yourself into the hands of" somebody else. You must be ready, willing, and able to open yourself up to that person, to expose yourself, to set yourself up, to drop whatever protective defenses you may have acquired to enter into an authentic relationship, naked and unarmed. To trust, of course, means to become vulnerable. Vulnerable means open to being hurt or used. Most of us can't let this happen. Most of us are "controllers" or manipulators. We aren't used to, nor willing to try, being under someone else's control or at another's disposal. Yet this is partly what love is all about.

Fromm says we have to accept four traits if the love thing is going to be real and give us pleasure. We have to know the other, respect the other, care for the other, and be responsible to the other. Knowing means more than intellectual knowledge: it means deep, intimate, personal knowing, and it often takes time. Take heed, you impetuous and impatient young lovers! Love at first sight is more a fantasy, a screenplay, than a reality. It rarely happens.

Respect means appreciation for the unique individuality and character of another person. It means you want him to become everything he can be. It means setting him up for fulfillment, and being willing to be an active partner in that process. It's plain hard work, and it calls for a degree of unselfishness.

Caring means concern-in-action. You can't just wish a person well. That's important, but you've got to be willing to do something in his best interests, in his behalf. You've got to show concern and act on it. It may mean protecting him, it may mean defending or helping or interceding for him. Whatever form it takes, it means *doing* something, actively and personally, to enhance the well-being of the one you love.

Responsibility is better spelled response-ability. It means you are able and willing to respond to the emotional needs of your loved one. It means seeing or sensing his needs and following through in trying to meet them. This is where most of us fall down on the job. We like the hugging or kissing, the sexual and sensual pleasures, but we don't all like to follow through with the hard part of it.

Fromm also cautions us against one-sided "love affairs." They don't exist. Love is a relationship, and as such, it involves two people at least. Each person in the relationship must give and get as much as the other. The words for this are mutuality and reciprocity, but they are rather cold and intellectual. Most simply, I must get as much out of this relationship as you do, and you also must get as much pleasure and satisfaction and comfort and joy as I do.

All of the above is probably right, maybe even true, but there is something about love that just can't be defined or even explained.

Abraham Maslow, a very loving and wise man, tells us that young people today have extracted a lot of the "juices" out of love. By claiming to know it, easily and cheaply, they claim to have had it all. Yet what many of them (and us) have done is to "desacralize" love, especially the sexual expression of it:

> These youngsters mistrust the possibility of values and virtues. They feel themselves swindled or thwarted in their lives. Most of them have, in fact, dopey parents whom they don't respect very much, parents who are quite confused themselves about values and who, frequently, are simply terrified of their children and never punish them or stop them from doing things that are wrong. So you have a situation where the youngsters simply despise their elders—often for good and sufficient reason. Such youngsters have learned to make a big generalization: They won't listen to anybody who is grown up, especially if the grown-up uses the same words which they've heard from the hypocritical mouth. . . .
>
> The youngsters have learned to reduce the person to the concrete object and to refuse to see what he might be or to refuse to see him in his symbolic values or to refuse to see him or her eternally. Our kids have desacralized sex, for example. Sex is nothing; it is a natural thing, and they have made it so natural that it has lost its poetic qualities in many instances, which means that it has lost practically everything.[1]

We don't mean anything religious or spiritual here, and neither does Maslow, at least not in the conventional sense of those terms. What has to be involved in love is some mystery, some feeling that even though we can't understand everything going on, it still feels good. There should be something about the person, about the relationship, that can't quite be identified, that we just can't put our finger on, that goes beyond words. True lovers know this and tend to enjoy the experience. Most of us would sit around and brood about the mystery: we've just got to make sense—mathematical and logical sense—out of everything we do. Pity, that!

To get a glimpse of why this is so, we have to dig into mythology.

---

1. Abraham Maslow, "Self-Actualization and Beyond," in James F. T. Bugental, *The Challenges of Humanistic Psychology*. (New York: McGraw-Hill Book Co., 1967), p. 284.

Rollo May helps us here. He reminds us that Eros, whom we call the god of love, was a puzzling creature. He wasn't human, but he wasn't quite divine. He was what the ancient Greeks called a *daimon*. Plato says it: "Eros is a daimon. He is neither mortal nor immortal, but a mean between the two. . . . He is the mediator between men and gods, and therefore in him all is bound together."

Rollo May defines the *daemonic* (or *daimonic*) as any natural function in the individual.

> which has the power of taking over the whole person. . . . Eros is the daemon which constitutes man's creative spirit, the drive that not only impels him to sexual union and to other forms of love, but also incites in him the yearning for knowledge and drives him to seek union with the truth, to become poet, or artist, or scientist. Sex and Eros, anger and rage, and the craving for power are daemonic and thus *either* creative or destructive.[2]

All this means that love and sex are extremely powerful forces in our lives. They are sources of sublime satisfaction and hellish frustrations—often at the same time. Most people who love know that they experience the fullest frustration and anger, even hatred, with the ones they love.

The opposite of love isn't hate; they go together and are complementary parts of the whole. The opposite of love is *indifference* or apathy. If love is deep feeling ("pathos") then its opposite is no feeling ("apathy"). Hate and love are parts of the same kind of involvement. This means that there's a tremendous amount of tension and conflict in a love relationship. It isn't all peace and calm and nice, gooey feelings; it may mean hurt and bother and upset and anxiety and even fear. But since it also means joy and fondness and pleasure and peace and Candyland, it's certainly well worth all the "bad" parts.

Love is often wild and unexplainable. It should be! Nothing is so unsatisfying as a placid, taken-for-granted relationship. I would join Maslow and May and Fromm and many, many real lovers in saying that to love is to know (and yet not know) a lot of wild and unpredictable, sensual and cognitive, joyous and unrehearsed, spontaneous and free kinds of feelings and experiences.

---

2. Quoted in Erich Fromm, "The Daemonic: Love & Death," in *Psychology Today,* Feb. 1968, pp. 16–17.

As a teacher and certainly as a therapist, there is nothing more important I can give my students and clients than this insight: Love, and love well. It can mean all the difference between a full or an empty life. Since "what the world needs now is love, sweet love," I wish you real love, wild and full and free and *warm! Take love*; take life!

Bibliography

Here are some of the works that have aided us in the preparation of this book of readings. We append them here for your further study.

Chapter One: The Crisis of Insignificance

Bugental, James F. T., *Challenges of Humanistic Psychology* (New York: McGraw-Hill Book Co., Inc., 1967).

Frankl, Viktor E., *Man's Search for Meaning* (New York: Washington Square Press, 1963).

Josephson, Eric, and Mary Josephson, eds., *Man Alone: Alienation in Modern Society* (New York: Dell Publishing Co., Inc., 1962).

May, Rollo, *Psychology and the Human Dilemma* (Princeton, N.J.: D. Van Nostrand Co., Inc., 1967).

Ruitenbeek, H. M., ed., *Psychoanalysis and Existential Philosophy* (New York: E. P. Dutton & Co., Inc., 1962).

Severin, Frank T., ed., *Humanistic Viewpoints in Psychology* (New York: McGraw-Hill Book Co., 1965).

Sutich, A. J., and M. A. Vich, eds., *Reading in Humanistic Psychology* (New York: The Free Press, 1969).

Vonnegut, Kurt, Jr., *Player Piano* (New York: Avon Books, 1967).

Chapter Two: The Nature of Man

Dobzhansky, Th., *Mankind Evolving* (New Haven, Conn.: Yale University Press, 1962).

Dubos, René, *So Human An Animal* (New York: Charles Scribner's Sons, 1968).

Hesse, Herman, *Siddhartha* (New York: New Directions Paperback, 1961).

Huxley, T. H., and J. Huxley, *Touchstone for Ethics* (New York: Harper & Bros., 1947).

Lamont, Corliss, *The Philosophy of Humanism* (New York: Frederick Ungar Publishing Co., 1965).

Maslow, Abraham, "Our Maligned Animal Nature," *Journal of Psychology,* Vol. 28 (1949), pp. 273–8.

Montagu, Ashley, *On Being Human* (New York: Hawthorn Books, Inc., 1966).

———, *The Biosocial Nature of Man* (New York: Grove Press, Inc., 1956).

Chapter Three: The Biosocial Experience

Boss, M., "Mechanistic and Holistic Thinking in Modern Medicine," *American Journal of Psychoanalysis,* Vol. 14, (1954), pp. 48–54.

Dobzhansky, Theodosius, *The Biology of Ultimate Concern* (New York: New American Library, 1967).

Dubos, René, *So Human An Animal* (New York: Charles Scribner's Sons, 1968).

Freud, Sigmund, *The Basic Writings of Sigmund Freud* (New York: The Modern Library, 1938).

Maslow, Abraham, *Motivation and Personality* (New York: Harper & Row, 1954).

Masters, W. H., and V. Johnson, *Human Sexual Response* (Boston: Little, Brown & Co., 1966).

Stoller, Robert J., *Sex and Gender* (New York: Science House, 1968).

Storr, Anthony, *Human Aggression* (New York: Atheneum Publishers, 1968).

Watts, Alan W., *Psychotherapy East and West* (New York: Ballantine Books, 1969).

Williams, R. J., *Biochemical Individuality* (New York: John Wiley & Sons, 1956).

Wooldridge, Dean E., *Mechanical Man: The Physical Basis of Intelligent Life* (New York: McGraw-Hill Paperbacks, Inc., 1968).

Chapter Four: The Emotional Self

Adler, Alfred, *Social Interest: A Challenge to Mankind* (New York: Capricorn Books, 1964).

Dollard, J., L. Doob, N. Miller, O. H. Mowrer, and R. Sears, *Frustration and Aggression* (New Haven, Conn.: Yale University Press, 1939).

Grier, W. H., and P. M. Cobbs, *Black Rage* (New York: Basic Books, Inc., 1968).

*Lorenz, Konrad, *On Aggression* (New York: Bantam Books, 1967).

Montagu, Ashley, *The Human Revolution* (New York: Bantam Books, 1965).

Schutz, William, *Joy: Expanding Human Awareness* (New York: Grove Press, Inc., 1967).

Siu, R. G. H., *The Tao of Science* (Cambridge, Mass.: M.I.T. Press, 1964).

Watts, Alan W., *The Book: On the Taboo Against Knowing Who You Are* (New York: Collier Books, 1967).

(Note: * denotes a book with an opposing viewpoint, but still one with which you ought to become familiar.)

Chapter Five: The Social Self

*Ardrey, Robert, *The Territorial Imperative* (New York: Atheneum Publishers, 1966).

Buber, Martin, *I and Thou* (New York: Charles Scribner's Sons, 1958).

Fromm, Erich, *The Art of Loving* (New York: Harper & Row, 1956).

Kropotkin, Petr, *Mutual Aid* (Boston: Porter Sargent, 1955).

Montagu, Ashley, *Darwin, Competition, and Cooperation* (New York: Schuman, 1952).

*Morris, Desmond, *The Naked Ape* (New York: McGraw-Hill Book Co., 1967).

(Note: * denotes a book with an opposing viewpoint, but one which we recommend so that you can gain multiple viewpoints.)

Chapter Six: The Working and Creative Self

Fabun, Don, *You and Creativity* (Beverly Hills, Calif.: Glencoe Press, 1968).

Fromm, Erich, *Escape From Freedom* (New York: Farrar & Rinehart, 1944).

Herzberg, Frederick, *et al., The Motivation to Work* (New York: John Wiley & Sons, 1959).

————, *Work and the Nature of Man* (Cleveland: World Publishing Co., 1966).

Kubie, L., "The Forgotten Man in Education," *Harvard Alumni Bulletin,* Vol. 56 (1953–54), pp. 349–53.

Lynd, R. S., *Knowledge for What?* (Princeton, N.J.: Princeton University Press, 1939).

Mayo, Elton, *The Social Problems of an Industrial Civilization* (Cambridge, Mass.: Harvard University, Division of Research, Graduate School of Business Administration, 1945).

Mills, C. Wright, *White Collar* (New York: A Galaxy Book, Oxford University Press, 1956).

Royce, Joseph R., *The Encapsulated Man* (Princeton, N.J.: D. Van Nostrand Co., Inc., 1964).

Tawney, R. H., *Religion and the Rise of Capitalism* (New York: Mentor Books, New American Library, 1955).

Weber, Max, *The Protestant Ethic and the Spirit of Capitalism* (New York: Charles Scribner's Sons, 1962).

Chapter Seven: The Self at Play

Berne, Eric, *Games People Play* (New York: Grove Press, Inc., 1964).

Caillois, R., *Man, Play and Games* (New York: The Free Press, 1961).

Denney, Reuel, *The Astonished Muse* (Chicago: University of Chicago Press, 1959).

Endelman, Robert, *Personality and Social Life* (New York: Random House, 1967).

Huizinga, J., *Homo Ludens: The Play Element in Culture* (Boston: Beacon Press, 1955).

Larrabee, E., and R. Meyersohn, eds., *Mass Leisure* (New York: The Free Press, 1958).

Wolfenstein, Martha, "The Emergence of Fun Morality," *Journal of Social Issues,* Vol. 7, No. 4, (1951), pp. 15–25.

Chapter Eight: Masking and Unmasking

Bugental, J. F. T., *The Search for Authenticity* (New York: Holt, Rinehart & Winston, 1965).

Cooper, D., ed., *To Free a Generation* (New York: Collier Books, 1968).

Fabun, Don, *The Children of Change* (Beverly Hills, Calif.: Glencoe Press, 1969).

Farber, J., *The Student as Nigger* (North Hollywood, Calif.: Contact Books, 1969).

Farber, S. M., and R. Wilson, eds., *The Potential of Women* (New York: McGraw-Hill Book Co., 1963).

Friedan, Betty, *The Feminine Mystique* (New York: Dell Publishing Co., 1963).

Goffman, Erving, *The Presentation of Self in Everyday Life* (Garden City, N.Y.: Doubleday Anchor Books, 1959).

Gregory, Dick, *The Shadow that Scares Me* (Garden City, N.Y.: Doubleday & Co., 1968).

Ittelson, W. H., and H. Cantril, *Perception: A Transactional Approach* (Garden City, N.Y.: Doubleday & Co., 1964).

Kunen, James, *The Strawberry Statement: Notes of a College Revolutionary* (New York: Avon Books, 1968).

Laing, Ronald D., *The Self and Others* (London: Tavistock Publications, Ltd., 1962).

Marden, C. F., and G. Meyer, *Minorities in American Society* (New York: American Book Co., 1968).

Newsweek Magazine, March 23, 1970. Entire issue devoted to Women's Liberation activities.

Shostrom, Everett, *Man, the Manipulator* (New York: Bantam Books, 1968).

Time Magazine, April 6, 1970. Entire issue devoted to emergence of the new Black Americans.

Yablonsky, Lewis, *The Hippie Trip* (New York: Pegasus Books, 1970).

Chapter Nine: The Self in Conflict

Arendt, Hannah, *The Human Condition* (Garden City, N.Y.: Doubleday Anchor Books, 1959).

Bellow, Saul, *Herzog* (Greenwich, Conn.: Fawcett Publications, 1965).

Camus, Albert, *The Rebel* (New York: Vintage Books, 1958).

——, *The Stranger* (New York: Vintage Books, 1946).

Laing, Ronald D., *The Divided Self* (London: Tavistock Publications, Ltd., 1960).

Maslow, Abraham, "Emotional Blocks to Creativity," *Journal of Individual Psychology,* Vol. 14 (1958), pp. 51–6.

Menninger, Karl, *Man Against Himself* (New York: Harvest Books, 1958).

Stephen, Karin, *The Wish to Fall Ill* (Cambridge: Cambridge University Press, 1960).

Chapter Ten: The Authentic Self

Berne, Eric, *Transactional Analysis in Psychotherapy* (New York: Grove Press, Inc., 1961).

Bugental, James F. T., "The Existential Crisis in Intensive Psychotherapy," *Psychotherapy* Vol. 2 (1965), pp. 16–20.

——, *The Search for Authenticity* (New York: Holt, Rinehart & Winston, 1965).

Eysenck, H. J., *Behavior Therapy and the Neuroses* (New York: Pergamon Press, 1960).

Gibb, J. R., "Climate for Trust Formation," in L. P. Bradford, J. R. Gibb, and K. D. Benne, eds., *T-Group Theory and Laboratory Method* (New York: John Wiley & Sons, 1964).

Glasser, William, *Reality Therapy* (New York: Harper & Row, 1962).

Jourard, Sidney, *Disclosing Man to Himself* (Princeton, N.J.: D. Van Nostrand Co., Inc., 1968).

Perls, F. S., R. Hefferline, and Paul Goodman, *Gestalt Therapy* (New York: The Julian Press, 1951).

Rogers, Carl R., "Toward a Science of the Person," in A. J. Sutich and Miles Vich, eds., *Readings in Humanistic Psychology* (New York: The Free Press, 1969).

Szasz, Thomas, *The Myth of Mental Illness* (New York: Hoeber Medical Div., Harper & Row, 1961).

Wolpe, J., *Psychotherapy by Reciprocal Inhibition* (Stanford, Calif.: Stanford University Press, 1958).

Chapter Eleven: The Transcending Self

Bucke, R. M., *Cosmic Consciousness* (New York: E. P. Dutton & Co., 1969).

Buhler, Charlotte, *Values in Psychotherapy* (New York: The Free Press, 1962).

Carey, J., *The College Drug Scene* (Englewood Cliffs, N.J.: Prentice-Hall Publishing Co., 1968).